CARMA SUTRA

The **auto-erotic** handbook

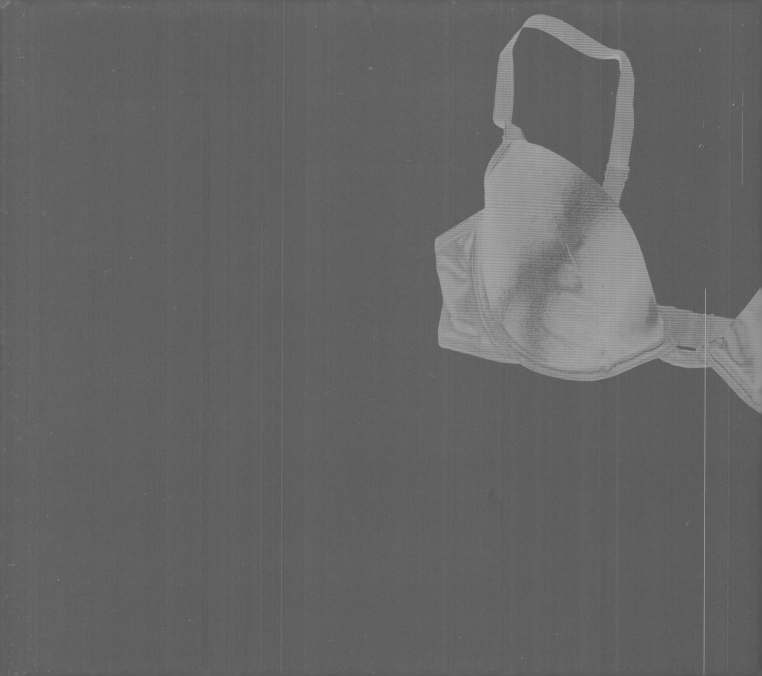

CARMA SUTRA

The **auto-erotic** handbook

A manual of **sex positions** for **in-car** entertainment

Alex Games & Esther Selsdon

First published in the United States by Dusk Books, 375 Hudson Street, New York, New York 10014.

PUBLISHER: **Carl Raymond**
EXECUTIVE MANAGING EDITOR: **Sharon Lucas**
EDITOR: **Brian Saliba**
ART DIRECTOR: **Dirk Kaufman**
MANAGING ART EDITOR: **Michelle Baxter**
PRODUCTION MANAGER: **Ivor Parker**

Copyright © iBall Press Limited 2006

A CIP catalog record for this book is available from the Library of Congress

ISBN-13: 978-0-7566-2461-3
ISBN-10: 0-7566-2461-4

Printed and bound in China.
05 06 07 08 09 10 9 8 7 6 5 4 3 2 1

This book was conceived, designed, and produced by
iBall Press Limited
The Old Candlemakers, West Street,
Lewes, East Sussex BN7 2NZ, UK

PUBLISHER: **Jason Hook**
CREATIVE DIRECTOR: **Peter Bridgewater**
ART DIRECTOR: **Sarah Howerd, Kevin Knight**
EDITORIAL DIRECTOR: **Caroline Earle**
SENIOR PROJECT EDITOR: **Stephanie Evans**
DESIGN: **Jo Hill, Tonwen Jones**
ILLUSTRATOR: **Ivan Hissey**
PICTURE RESEARCHER: **Katie Greenwood**
CONSULTANT: **Richard Porter**
ADDITIONAL TEXT: **Viv Croot, Jane Moseley**

For more information about iBall Press Ltd, go to www.ivy-group.co.uk

Contents

Introduction

There is no doubt that had Vatsyayana, author of the original *Kama Sutra*, been compiling his great sex manual in the 21st century, he would have produced some *shlokas* on sex in cars. After all, we spend more time in our cars than anywhere else. Alas, he died several centuries before the first Model T rolled off the assembly line, so it was not part of his agenda. The same can be said for Li T'ung Hsuan, author of the eponymous Tao text, *T'ung Hsuan Tzu* (8th century); Sheik Nefwazi, author of the Arabic love guide, *The Perfumed Garden* (15th century); and the poet Kalyanamalla, author of the *Ananga Ranga* (15th–16th centuries).

So, the *Carma Sutra* has been created to fill the gap. It brings these traditional wisdoms up to date, as we feel sure that vehicular sex would have warranted a complete subsection in any ancient book of love, had the erotic thrill delivered by torque and thrust been known at the time.

Carma Sutra begins with general advice, tips, warnings, precautions, and an evaluation of the merits of the two types of transmission: stick shift and automatic. To get you started, Your First Ride introduces you to the world of carmic love. If you've never had great sex in a car before, you need the lowdown on the possibilities—and pitfalls—of making out in a vehicle (front, back, cargo area, hood, and trunk). What are the pre-date requirements? Are you prepared for safe sex? How well do you know the ins and outs of the car? The last thing you want to do is kill the passion by setting off the alarm, activating an airbag, or

A note for beginners >

> Don't worry if you happen to be a carmic virgin. For some, just reading the *Carma Sutra* is your key to advanced sensual pleasure, because it evokes the smell of the upholstery and the prospect of the open road.

inadvertently releasing the parking brake. Acquainting yourself with the features and specification of your vehicle type (sedan, hatchback, or convertible) can save you the embarrassment of getting caught—literally—with your pants down.

Once you have mastered the basics, move on to Advanced Driving, where you'll learn how to release the carmic potential of specific models. We cater to all tastes, shapes, and sizes. Each spread pairs the vehicle specifications with a carefully chosen sexual position—and suitable alternatives—that will show you how to get the ride of your life. We've taken into account cockpit layout; available head, hip, and legroom; and seat configuration, as well as tips on how to make the best of additional features such as cup holders, collapsible steering wheels, and moonroofs.

For quick reference, we've included the Crash Test Carma Sutra, an at-at-glance visual guide to all the positions suggested for your auto-erotic experience. As your confidence grows, you will want to try out variations, even evolve new carmic positions. And, since no body can run on desire alone, our Carma Sutra includes a section on Maintenance and Troubleshooting—for you and your vehicle.

Sit back and enjoy the ride!

1. Technical Information

This section covers basic technical and safety information that is applicable to all makes and models that appear later in the manual. Don't be tempted to skip it because you're in a rush to get down to business. Remember that thorough research and good preparation always pay off.

The first pages explain the recommended carmic positions, review the ancient sex manuals that inspired them, and discuss why they were included. A thematic index of positions will steer you around the manual and help you find the best positions for you, your partner, and your car.

Next, we introduce you to the two transmission types—automatic and stick shift—and outline the principles, pros, and cons of each option. Even if you are already committed one way or the other, don't be afraid to experiment. Those of you who learned to drive on an automatic will need a few hours of practice to be able to handle the more physically challenging demands of a stick shift, but anyone who learned on a manual will have no problem adjusting to an automatic. It's a good idea to get used to both, as you and your partner may drive different models.

Finally, Taking Precautions lays down the ground rules for the practice of safe *Carma Sutra*. It covers basic legal and mechanical points as well as simple safety procedures and useful condom storage advice. It looks at seatbelts and shows how they can extend beyond their conventional preventative role and contribute to carmic enjoyment. A section on airbags teaches you what to do if you find yourself in an accidental deployment situation.

Suitable Positions Explained

⚠ The positions suggested in this book have been carefully selected to fit the dimensions of specific car models. We have made every effort to ensure that you and your partner will fit, but if one or both of you are extra tall or short, or in other ways non-standard, you may need to make some adjustments on the fly.

The original *Kama Sutra* listed 64 configurations in eight groups of eight; the *Ananga Ranga* groups its range into five categories; while *The Perfumed Garden*, more of a hybrid model, offers 11 basic positions plus 20 or so variations, all of them imports; and the Taoist tradition pares the range down to four basic models with a variety of options. This gives you many choices, though not all of them are suitable for vehicular adaptation.

You will find a repertoire of sitting positions (mainly for use in the front seat), kneeling positions (for cramped back seats or bench-style front seats), lying positions (for generous back seats and the cargo area), and standing positions for use with a convertible, or vehicles equipped with a moon/sunroof. Take your time, practice, and get to know the dimensions of your vehicle and the various ways its seats and cargo area can be configured. These positions are suggestions only (listed in the Positions panel), so don't be afraid to experiment and customize for yourself.

Tips >

> Bag a few thrills by borrowing a friend's car for the evening.
> If you want to try something luxurious, but don't have the budget, consider renting, or booking a test drive. This gives you the chance to handle the speed and glamor of, for example, the Mazda MX-5 Miata (*see page 34*), without making a commitment or trashing your comfortable long-term relationship with your reliable old Dodge. Always clean up after yourselves.

Pre-date Checklist

☐ It pays to study your car. New models may have been updated; even minor changes and adjustments can make all the difference in your love life.

☐ *Carma Sutra* beginners should check the car for sharp or corroded areas.

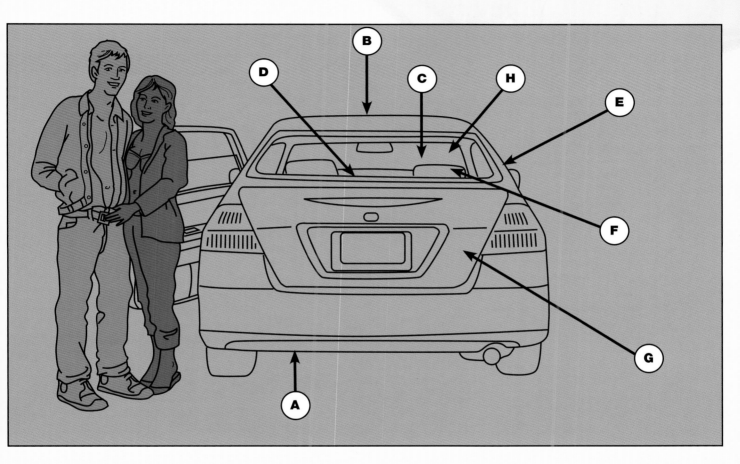

1.1 Carma queries for you and your car. **(A)** Is the suspension good? **(B)** Fixed top or convertible? Sun- or moonroof? **(C)** Tinted windows? **(D)** Stick shift or automatic? Central console or column-mounted gearshift? **(E)** 2-doors or 4? **(F)** Bucket or bench seating? Folding or removable? **(G)** Trunk or hatchback? **(H)** How much headroom?

Automatic Transmission

⚠️ **Precautions:** Avoid using the gearshift as a hand grip during carmic climax, especially the T-bar style. Putting your car in Drive in the heat of the moment could kill the mood.

The majority of today's cars have automatic transmissions (84% in North America), so most of us are used to having the right gear selected for us. Some automatics offer an automanual mode, which simulates manual shifting; a few have CVT (continuously variable transmission)—often more responsive than standard automatic.

In carmic terms what's important is the extra space around the driver and passenger seat afforded by automatic transmission. Although the transmission block between driver and passenger has been replaced in most modern cars with a console for storing drinks or a pop-up DVD screen, this is usually upholstered and you can sprawl over it quite easily.

The automatic gearshift will be mounted either on the steering column or on the console between the seats, where it is usually a chunky T-bar or, as in the Toyota Camry, a stumpy club that fits snugly into the hand. The T-bar is easier to work around and less uncomfortable if you inadvertently sit on it, but the Camry-style gearshift is usually positioned forward of the seat edge and tucked tidily over on the driver's side, where it will be easy to avoid.

Positions >

If you have a column-mounted gear selector and a bench seat, go for side-by-side, horizontal positions such as:
❤ Crab Embrace
❤ **Transverse Lute (as shown)**

If the selector is console mounted and you have to deal with bucket seats go for sitting positions such as:
❤ **Goat on the Tree (as shown)**
❤ The Seducer

These are recommendations only. What you can do depends on the size of the seats, and your own physical specs.

Pros >

+ more relaxing drive will deliver you to your date in a mellow mood
+ more room in the front of the car
+ comfortable transmisson block

Cons >

− gearshift can be knocked out of place as a result of carmic exertions
− cannot be push-started, so if the battery dies, you are stuck

Top cars for automatic fun >

> BMW 750i
> Aston Martin DB9
> Lexus LS430
> Cadillac Escalade
> Range Rover Sport
> Cadillac Coupe De Ville
> Rolls-Royce Phantom
> Ferrari 599 GTB Fiorano F1
> Hummer H1
> Lincoln Town Car

Hazards >

A Steering wheel: could cramp your style—adjust it up as high as possible
B Electronic seats: triggering the memory control could cause unwanted movement
C Doors: best left open for this position, but park discreetly, and expect drafts

Manual Transmission

⚠ Precautions: Heavy vibrations can cause the stick to jump. If it goes into neutral and the parking brake is off, you could find yourself moving rather faster than planned… Verify that the parking brake is on. Park in first gear or reverse, so if the parking brake does get knocked out of position, the car won't roll.

Stick shift or automatic? It is one of the most basic decisions that confronts car owners. Automatic fans sneer at such an old-fashioned, hands-on approach; stick-shift fans claim that watching your partner effortlessly master two tons of screaming metal using only smooth wrist action and nimble footwork is a turn-on in itself. Remember Richard Gere grinding the gears in the manual Lotus Esprit Turbo in *Pretty Woman*? He couldn't drive a stick shift; Julia Roberts could. How sexy is that?

With a stick shift, you must choose when to change gears, engaging the clutch pedal with your foot and moving the gearshift up or down through four, five, or six gears. The problem for carmic practitioners is that most gearshifts are floor-mounted as part of the transmission block between the front seats. They tend to stick out at awkward angles, though modern ones are usually short and stubby. Models with the gearshift mounted on the steering column are ideal for carmic purposes as they allow for front-bench seating, one of the seductive features of the old '50s Bel-Airs that once cruised the streets of every small town full of highschool sweethearts joined at the hip.

Alternatively, look for gearshifts mounted on the steering wheel itself—as in Formula One cars (though this might characterize you as more of a car geek than a carmic enthusiast).

Top cars for stick-shift fun >

> VW Golf
> Chevrolet Bel Air
> Lancia Fulvia
> Ford Escort XR3i
> Mini Cooper
> Ford Thunderbird
> Mazda MX5
> Audi Quattro
> Saab 9–3
> Fiat 500

Positions >

The size of the car, and the position of the gearshift and parking brake dictate what positions are possible in the front seats. Don't kneel in the driver's footwell. You will get tangled in the pedals and may inadvertently engage the clutch. If the car is in neutral, and the parking brake insecure, you could get carried away. Try the following:

♥ Sporting of the Swan (man resting on his arms)
♥ **The Rising Position (as shown)**
♥ Lotus Position

Pros >

+ puts you in control
+ hones dexterity
+ keeps both hands busy so you are not tempted to start carma while in motion

Cons >

– more strenuous driving experience could leave the driver all tuckered out
– less room in the driver's seat area
– fewer front-seat options

Hazards >

A Parking brake: if this is on top of or beside the transmission block, beware—it is vulnerable to unexpected release
B Radio: avoid impact, unless you can go with any beat
C Horn: can attract unwanted attention
D Vinyl seats: slippery when wet

Taking Precautions

⚠ Precautions: It sounds obvious, but do not attempt any of the carmic activity suggested in this book while driving, not even Auparishtaka (*see page 60*). If you are being driven, that is a different matter, but it's best to leave it to the professionals (a New York cab, London taxi, or chauffeured stretch limo—*see gatefolds 1 and 2*). If a friend or other amateur driver is at the wheel, he or she might be too easily distracted and attempt to join in.

Preparations

> Make sure the gas tank is full enough to get you there and back. It may be an appealing carmic roleplay to fantasize that you have run out of gas, but the reality is that one of you will have to walk miles in the dark with the gas can, or you'll have to call for help. Either of these scenarios may make the adventure memorable for all the wrong reasons.

> Always practice safe sex. Keep a good supply of condoms in the lockable glove compartment so that you are never caught short. Take them out before things heat up and keep them on hand or in an extendable cupholder. Alternatively, tuck the condoms in the sunglasses holder that comes standard in some models (in the roof space between the front seats). If you reach for the condoms and find only your sunglasses, put them on nonchalantly as if this was your intention all along.

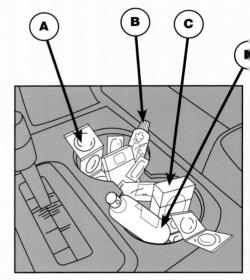

1.2 Use cup holders for carmic requisites **(A)** condoms; **(B)** lubricating gel; **(C)** tissues; **(D)** breath freshener.

Seatbelts

> Always buckle up while riding to your destination, but once you've arrived why not turn necessity into invention? Don't unbuckle the minute you come to a halt, take the opportunity to try a little safe bondage. If you are the driver, explore what it is like to be out of control for a while; keep your seat belt on while your passenger applies foreplay. Most cars come with standard three-point inertial belts. Unbuckling each other slowly and letting the slack slide through your hand can be fun.

Airbags

> Front seat airbags are mandatory in modern cars, and side-impact and curtain airbags often come as options. Sensors in the front of the car detect sudden deceleration when the car crashes, and spark the ignition of the gas canister in the airbag. The bag then deploys, filling with nitrogen. This all happens in about 30 milliseconds. Bags begin to deflate through pressure relief vents immediately after deployment. Although they are designed to deploy only when the car is in motion, like all mechanical devices they can go wrong, especially if the car overheats or bounces too much. If you do set them off, just wait for them to deflate. Open the windows as soon as you can because the car will fill with a fine white dust. This is only cornstarch or talcum powder, used as a lubricant, but it is not suitable for carmic activities and can aggravate allergies.

WARNING >

> Check local laws to find out when and where you can go carmic legally. In some places you might be restricted to your own driveway. This may not deliver an adrenalin rush, but rules are rules.

Hazards >

A Gauges: check all levels to avoid running dry
B Airbags: avoid impact or intense movements, which can activate them
C Doors: before leaning, pressing, or pushing against doors, be sure that they are fully closed and locked

At the Carwash

⚠ **Precautions: If you and your partner are hand-washing the car, do not use harsh detergents and make sure the water is not too hot. If utilizing an automatic carwash, check how long it takes, and avoid the full service version (operatives will hand-dry the car, affording them a good view of everything you are doing). Don't go to the same carwash every week.**

It's vital to feel clean and fresh before that all-important date, so why not turn the carwash into something more exciting by doing it together—what's better than sharing a shower with your partner and your car? Wet clothes look hot, and it is relatively easy for the man to achieve a rear entry position as the woman bends over the bodywork to wax and polish. The job can take as long as you want; all that rubbing will produce a brilliant finish.

Utilizing an automated carwash requires a more fast and furious approach and is an ideal way to spice up your sex life if you both have very full schedules. Choose an exterior wash option, where the car passes through a timed, pre-set washing cycle. Either go for a front seat position (*see page 24*), or make a quick transfer into the back. The Raised Feet Posture is recommended as it is a position that stimulates the G-spot to bring on the female orgasm very quickly, and in the carwash time is not on your side. The woman lies on her back and draws her knees up to her chin. The man enters from a kneeling position and rests on her legs. He is also in position to look up and check on the car's progress through the system. Allow time to scramble back into the front seats.

Pre-date Checklist

- Dirty up the car a little beforehand so that the washing takes longer.
- Don't wear your best clothes, and have towels handy in the car.
- One of you can get into the back seat to prepare before you drive into the carwash.
- Remove the front seat headrests to make it easier to climb from the back into the front seats.

MAJOR HAZARD Don't try hand wash on very low-slung cars as you can damage your back. In the carwash, don't be tempted to get out mid-cycle. The scrubbers rotate at 100 to 500 rpm, turning their soft cloth strips into lashes that will whip you senseless, and the high-speed jets pump out water at a pressure of up to 1000 lb/square inch, which will knock you off your feet.

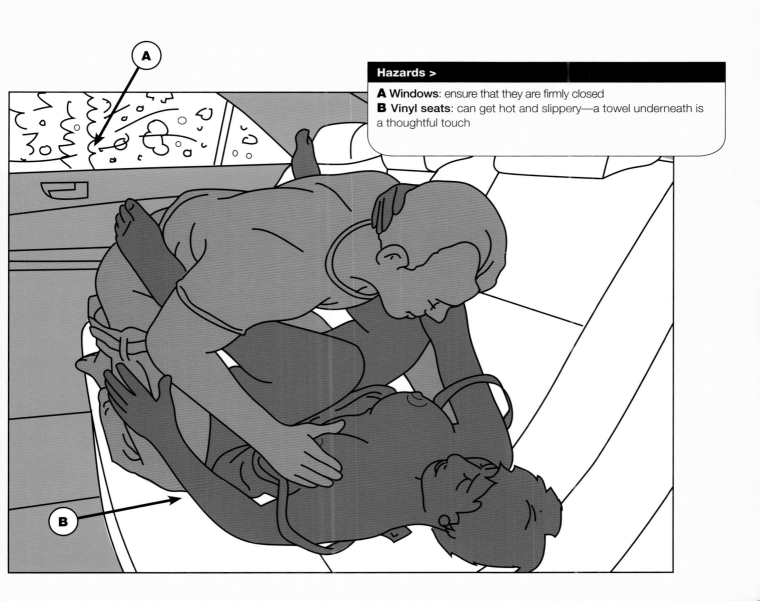

A Windows: ensure that they are firmly closed
B Vinyl seats: can get hot and slippery—a towel underneath is a thoughtful touch

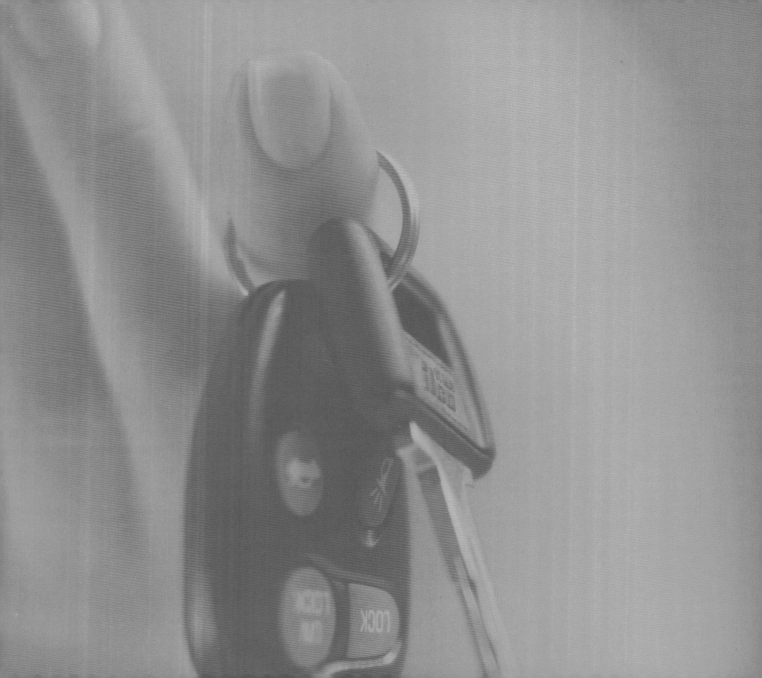

2. Your First Ride

Everybody remembers the first time. All that hard studying and those nerve-wracking practice sessions, and the sheer relief of actually passing one of life's milestones (especially if you've had to make several attempts at it). Then you are on your own. It is at once exhilarating and a little scary.

That's why we've designed this section of the *Carma Sutra* to ease you into the driver's seat, help you hone your handling skills, find your own particular driving style, and discover whether you are built for comfort or speed. Enough with the innuendo, already; this is a serious, practical manual about enjoying sex in—or even on—cars. We don't need the thrust and lubrication wordplay. You get the picture.

We'll start by looking at the opportunities for sex presented by all cars, regardless of make or model. Not all of our readers have their own car yet; you may have rented one especially for the occasion, or have just gotten your hands on the wheel of a friend's car (without the friend). Either way, this handy, introductory guide will provide you with the basic instructions you need to handle classic positions and maneuvers inside a variety of vehicles. From warming up the engine (sorry) and what it's like to be in the driver's seat, to the advantages of back-seat driving and the private pleasures of the trunk. For those of you who are just fooling around in the parking lot, or who are stuck in Driver's Ed 101, we offer the across-the-hood option, which can be successfully achieved on most vehicles, regardless of your driving skill.

This section finishes with an in-depth look at how to enjoy the best sex in three popular kinds of automobile: the sedan, the hatchback, and the convertible. Ladies and gentlemen, start your engines!

All Revved Up

⚠ **Precautions: Be sure that both of you know how far you want to take things. Provide condoms, stowed in the lockable glove compartment or overhead sunglasses storage.**

Just as eager novice drivers tend to over-rev the engine when they start up, inexperienced lovers can be too impatient to get down to it, and miss out on the essential warm-up that is foreplay. Unless you are already extremely pleased to see each other, foreplay is essential. It gets the blood flowing, initiates lubrication, heightens the senses, and prepares the body for sex. This is particularly important for practitioners of the *Carma Sutra* because you'll be working in confined spaces, and if one or both of you isn't ready, it can result in discomfort or cramping. The last thing you want is to have to call AAA to get you untangled.

The original *Kama Sutra* regarded embracing, kissing, pressing, and marking or scratching with nails as essential preparations for love, and all of these can easily be done in almost any type of car except a Formula One racer. Standing embraces such as the Twining of a Creeper or Climbing a Tree won't work (although seasoned practitioners of the *Carma Sutra* with a fine sense of balance may want to try them in a convertible), so concentrate on the touching, piercing, rubbing, and pressing embraces, all of which put you in a great position for kissing. The *Kama Sutra* lists many variants of the kiss—the bent kiss, the clasping kiss, etc.—and several styles (moderate, contracted, pressed, and soft). Experiment with all of them.

Unless you have a bench seat in the front, the transmission block will restrict your ability to embrace and kiss, so you might want to move to the back seat before you start. Electric windows can be operated without starting the engine. Lowering them a little will help to prevent steam-up.

Tips >

> In many modern cars, the CD player will remain active even when the engine is off, so you can set the mood with some suitable music.

> The courtesy light in most cars will fade out gently, so don't spoil the mood by switching it off abruptly.

MAJOR HAZARD Some car alarms are overly sensitive. Keyless entry systems that feature electronic keypads on the door can help you avoid accidentally setting off your car alarm, which will cool your ardor and attract unwanted attention.

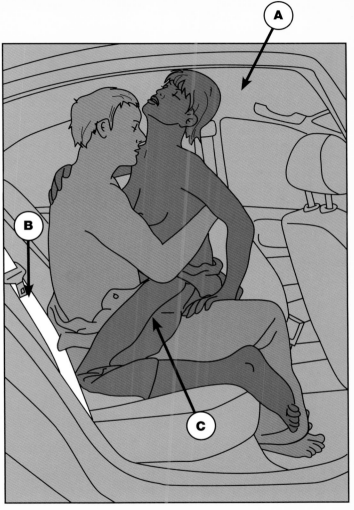

2.1 (A) Headroom may be restricted in the back of the car; **(B)** avoid entanglement with seatbelts, unless you want to use them; **(C)** wear clothing that can be easily removed.

In the Driver's Seat

⚠ Precautions: Do not try this in a GT390 Mustang Fastback, the kind Steve McQueen drove. Hot rod bucket seats are for one person only. The passenger's job in this car is to admire the driver's peerless handling and cornering skills. This can be an aphrodisiac in itself, but you will have to move over to satisfy your lust. Many cars have interior controls to adjust side mirrors. These controls can be kicked out of position, so make sure you check the alignment of your mirrors before driving off afterward.

A lot depends on headroom and the configuration of your front seats. Most modern cars have two individual bucket seats separated by the transmission arch. In some models, this is disguised as an arm rest with a storage compartment, but it usually sticks up too far for comfort, and only ends up getting in the way. Deferred lust is often much more fun than easy access, and you can always move around to the back seat when you can't contain yourselves any longer. However, if you are both slim and lithe, try the Goat on the Tree (pictured). The man sits in the driver's seat, and the woman lowers herself onto his lap with her back to him, gently rocking back and forth. She can hold onto the steering wheel (being careful to avoid honking the horn), while his hands are free to stimulate her.

Alternatively, move to the passenger seat, which usually reclines further, and try *The Perfumed Garden*'s Tenth Position. The woman lies back and the man kneels between her thighs (there should be plenty of room in the seat well). She slides her legs up over his hips, resting her feet on the dashboard, and squeezes. He leans forward, grips the top edge of the seat, and rocks them back and forth.

Pre-date Checklist

☐ Push seats as far back as you can. Standard seats can move 7–9 inches.

☐ If you have a telescopic, tilting steering wheel, push it as far out of the way as possible.

☐ Clear any garbage, CDs, books etc. from the floor around the seat.

☐ If you are planning to attempt the Tenth Position, adjust headrests so that there is enough room between them and the seat back.

Back-seat Driving

⚠️ **Precautions: Avoid this type of maneuver in a 2-door model as clambering in and out will kill the mood. Vehicles with rear-opening doors are the best of all. Some models have back seats that are set slightly higher than the front (one is the Hyundai Accent) to give passengers a better view. This will restrict your headroom if you are attempting a kneeling position.**

The back seat is the traditional makeout area, so embrace it. Head- and legroom are restricted (most modern back seats offer about 10 less inches of legroom and an inch or so less headroom than the front; in the Toyota Camry the legroom difference is only 3.4 inches).

Back seats are usually benches split on the 60:40 ratio, with adjustable armrests. This gives you an area roughly the size of a narrow single bed, room enough to try the Variant Yawning Position (pictured). The woman lies on her back, draws her legs up, and pushes her feet against the underside of the roof and her calves on the man's upper arms. He uses the basic missionary position, but is partially supported by her thighs. If either of you is too tall for this, fold down the back seats that open into the trunk, and try the Turning Position. The woman lies on her back, knees bent and legs apart, and the man begins with the standard missionary position, with his legs between hers. Then he gradually rotates 180 degrees without withdrawing, until he is facing her feet. This relies on better-than-average upper arm strength from him, but is very restful for her.

MAJOR HAZARD Central locking is a feature that prevents back doors from being opened if the driver's door is locked. If your car has central locking, you'll have to climb back into the front seat to get out. Many models feature cigar lighters in the back; they pack a 12-volt punch so don't accidentally turn one on.

Tips >

> Pull front seats as far forward as possible to maximize available space, leaning them forward, if possible.
> Stow condoms and anything else you will need in the map pouches on the back of the front seats.

2.4 (A) The driver will probably run his mouth throughout your performance; **(B)** likewise, the meter will run until you reach your destination; **(C)** would-be passengers may try to enter if you get stuck in traffic; **(D)** be prepared for unexpected U-turns.

London Taxi

⚠️ **Precautions:** If you've already enjoyed a ride in a New York cab, you'll find that being transported in a London Hackney Carriage, usually a black LTI TX1, is an altogether different experience. You'll have more legroom, but the driver will also have a much better view of what's going on.

To hail a cab, just stretch out an arm, shout "Taxi!", and you'll have a green light for *Carma Sutra* UK-style. The high-roofed London cab—55 inches, no less—with its luxurious suspension and wide passenger bench, offers the perfect stage for any performance. So if you've just caught a performance of *Cabaret* on the West End and are feeling a little "Sally Bowles," you're in luck! Historically, the roofs of London cabs had to be high enough to accommodate a man wearing a bowler hat. You even could hold a small orgy, complete with members of the chorus line and theater critics taking notes in the rear-facing seats, if that's your idea of a night on the town.

The optimum *Carma Sutra* pose for the London cab is the Crab Embrace (pictured). The woman lies on the long passenger bench (a towel will help you avoid slippage, and act as a cushion for the spine from the seatbelt slots) and wraps her bent-like-a-crab leg around the man's hips as he supports himself on his hands. Or you could opt for the Extended Crab Claw position, whereby the woman raises one leg almost over the man's shoulder.

The London cabbie may not be as free-thinking as his New York counterpart, but since they are always claiming to have had someone famous in the back of their cab they won't mind you having someone a little less famous on the seat. You may want to ask him to "step outside" for a while during the Cabaret act, but make sure he realizes that you are asking for discretion and not a round of fisticuffs.

MAJOR HAZARD It's a good idea to turn off the intercom so the driver can't hear you, otherwise your cries of "further up" and "move to the right" could be misinterpreted. And nothing spoils an evening like being charged for a ride from Holborn to Oxford Street via Glasgow. Passion should take a back seat when calculating a cab fare.

Tip >

> When confronted with a large denomination, taxi drivers aren't legally obliged to give change. They have the right to bill you at your home address, so be on the money or you may have to give out more details than you'd like.

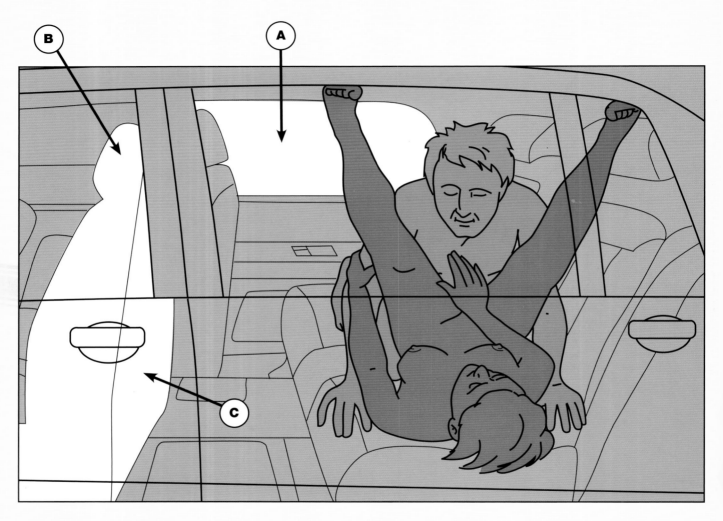

2.5 (A) Avoid banging your feet on the window, which may attract attention; **(B)** push the front seats forward; **(C)** use the map pouches on the back of the seats to store condoms or other carmic requisites.

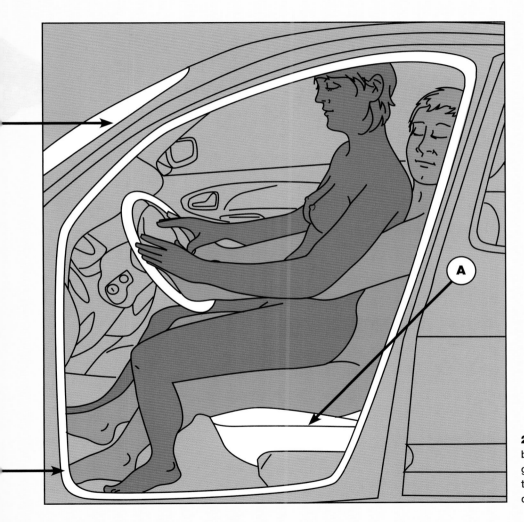

2.2 (A) Move the seats or bench back as far as possible; **(B)** tinted glass will help keep you focused on the action, **(C)** though leaving the door open prevents steam-up.

New York Taxi

⚠️ **Precautions:** The main advantage that the yellow New York taxi holds over its black London counterpart is the driver. He (or, if you are very lucky, she) will have seen it all before, so you can do whatever you like without feeling self-conscious. In fact, the driver will probably be happy to help out if you need a hand with anything. Make sure you tip generously, and remember that you can do what you like in their cabs, but if you leave the door open the drivers go crazy.

Rest assured that New York cab drivers have seen it all before, so throw any modesty or self-consciousness out of the window (but not your gum, litter, or underwear). He or she may well be happy to join in or at least administer plenty of advice, should you require assistance. Discretion is their forte—it is part of the training. The security partition ensures privacy and safety, and it is wise to request that the rear air-conditioning or heater be turned on in advance, depending on the season.

Now, down to business. How much bang do you get for your buck in what is likely to be a 3-year-old Crown Vic? It seats six (though it is a challenge to find a driver who will allow more than four passengers), but the place to be is definitely in the rear, with its generous 37.8 inches of headroom, 38 inches of leg room, and 60.3 inches of shoulder room. The passenger bench is generally leather- or vinyl-clad, like some of the passengers conveyed upon it, and is designed to make things—like money, cell phones, or condoms—fall out of your pockets before you embark on your *Carma Sutra* journey, so beware. Seats can be slippery, too, so instruct your driver to go easy on the corners and not to brake too sharply.

The position of choice for the iconic Crown Victoria is the White Tiger, a rear-entry position many women find extremely stimulating. The woman positions herself on the seat first, balancing on her knees and elbows, and raises her spread thighs to accommodate her kneeling partner. He can then clasp her waist with one hand while stimulating her with the other. The view from the rear is pretty exciting (for the man, at least).

 MAJOR HAZARD It is illegal to have sex in a public place in New York—and that includes taxi cabs. Always ask your cab driver's permission before embarking on any carmic fun in the back seat. And if you pull up next to NYC's finest, you'd better have a good explanation handy.

Tips >

> NY taxis all have air-conditioning, so there's no need to get all steamed up.
> There isn't a huge amount of room across the seats, so if you are particularly tall, energetic, or athletic, be prepared for grazed elbows.
> Bear in mind that the back seat of a cab has likely had thousands of passengers. So if you're a germophobe, you might want to keep your pants on.

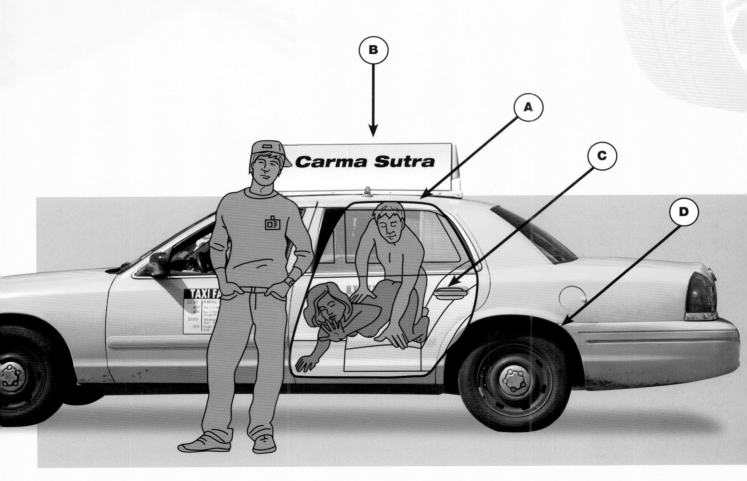

2.3 (A) Generous headroom; **(B)** billboard may draw attention of passers-by; **(C)** sticky seats; **(D)** screaming tires mask any noise.

Top cars for front seat space

> **Nissan Maxima**
legroom 44.8"/headroom 40.5"
> **Infiniti I35**
legroom 43.9"/headroom 40.5"
> **Volvo V70**
legroom 42.6"/headroom 39.3"
> **Ford Crown Victoria**
legroom 42.5"/headroom 39.4"
> **Buick Park Avenue**
legroom 42.4"/headroom 39.8"
> **Chevrolet Impala**
legroom 42.2"/headroom 39.2"

Positions >

If you enjoy a tight squeeze, try:
♥ **Goat on the Tree (as shown)**
♥ The Tenth Position

Bench-seat Driving

If you have a bench seat in the front—as found in many a pick-up truck, any of the Chrysler K cars, and early-model Chevy Impalas—you can snuggle up close to your partner without interruption. This will allow you to use any of the positions suggested for back seats or cargo areas. Bench seats are usually accompanied by a column-mounted gearshift. Avoid knocking the shifter out of position during carmic activity.

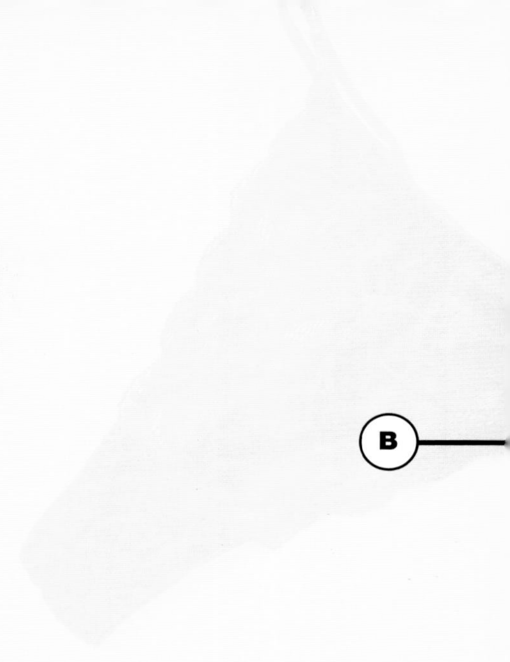

B

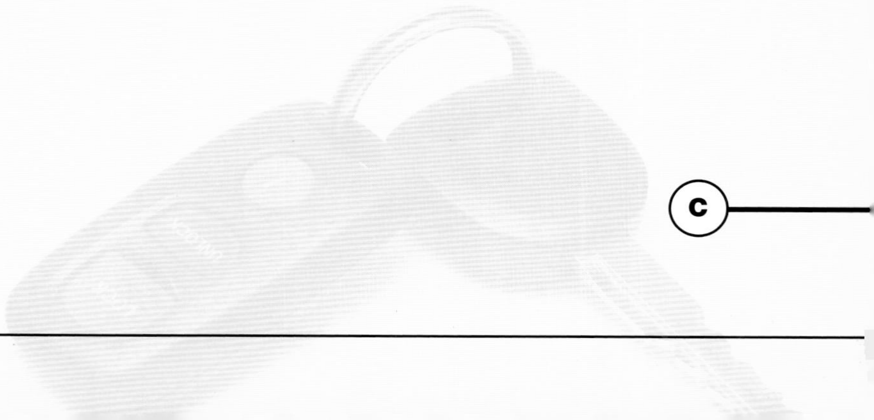

C

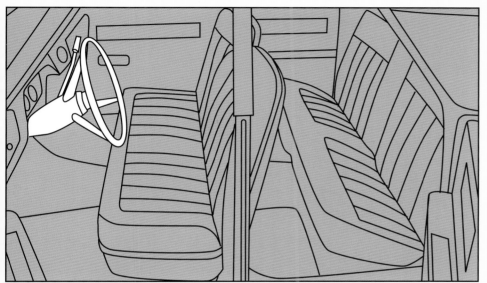

Lincoln Continental

Forget the elegant lines, the luxurious interior, and the 7-liter V8 Ford MEL engine. This car boasts rear-hinged back doors, which allow easy access from front seat to back. Known as suicide doors, they are hinged to open outward as on the Lincoln Continental (1961–9). Rear suicide doors make it really easy to leap out of the front seat and into the back in an almost seamless movement. Some new models (the Saturn Ion Coupe, Mazda RX8) have suicide half-doors on the back, which can only be opened after the front doors have been. This affords you some privacy, but it also means that you cannot get out of the car until one of you has climbed back into a front seat.

2.6 Ease of access and bench seats in the front and back make the Lincoln Continental ideal for swingers.

Across the Hood

⚠ Precautions: Wait for the hood to cool down if it has been a hot day, or if the engine has just been turned off (unless you are driving a rear-engined VW Type 4). Check ground clearance (at least 6 inches) in order to avoid damaging the suspension.

This is a spontaneous move for those who can't wait to get into the car, let alone get a room, or for those who don't actually have a car but love the smell of gasoline. Head for the parking lot and assess the potential. Most modern sedans have sloping hoods and are difficult either to lean against or sprawl across, so look for an SUV, an off-roader, or an old-school luxury sedan.

You need height and/or width. Tall cars like the Jeep Commander (71.9 inches) or the Land Rover LR3 (74.1 inches) are ideal, and very solid, as they are built to withstand a challenge—including a rhino charge. Use them to execute an athletic position like Driving the Peg Home (pictured), which is traditionally performed against a wall. The woman perches on the edge of the hood, facing the man, legs apart, feet resting on the fender. The man stands in front of her (he may have to bend his knees or stand on the fender, depending on his height). She then wraps her legs and arms around him to keep the couple in congress. Our carmic variation means that he does not have to support her weight, but he must hold her close to him in order to keep her from sliding backward as he thrusts.

If the hood is broad and flat, you could try the Top. The man lies flat across the hood (spreading his weight evenly) and the woman sits astride him, raises her legs clear of his body and swivels around. Any one of the big square-hooded vintage Volvo 200 series (nicknamed "the brick") would be ideal for this. Or, for a classier ride, try the Maserati Quattroporte Sport GT, or the iconic Jaguar E-type, a sure-to-impress 184 inches long, and most of that a one-piece hood. The E-type is only 48 inches high, and a ridge runs down the center of the hood, so this option is more about style than comfort.

MAJOR HAZARD As it may not be your car, you will not be able to check that the parking brake is on. Be aware that many car alarms are set off by external motion.

Pre-date Checklist
☐ Men may need socks to protect shins against fenders. Women should avoid heeled shoes, which could catch in the front grill.
☐ Go for a mud-spattered car if there is a choice; it may dirty your clothes but will provide more traction.

Top cars for hood fun >
> Willys Overland Jeep
> Land Rover LR3
> Jaguar E-type
> Volvo 240
> Chrysler 300C
> Maserati Quattroporte
> Mercedes GL450
> Aston Martin DB9 Volante
> Lincoln Town Car
> Honda Ridgeline

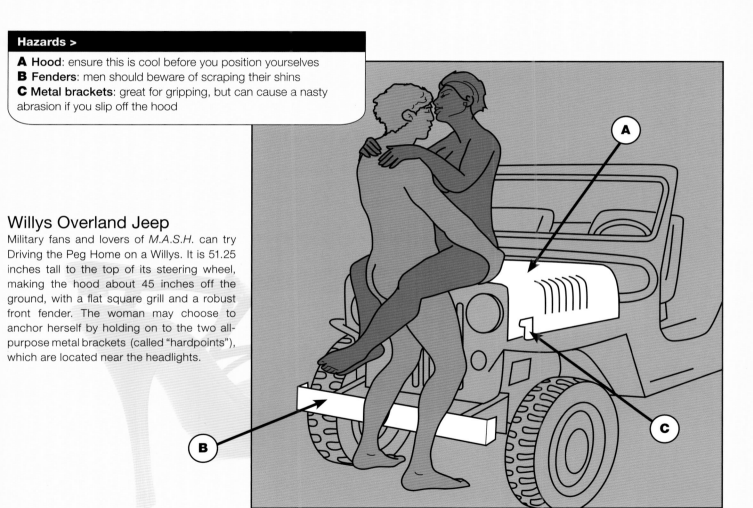

Willys Overland Jeep

Military fans and lovers of *M.A.S.H.* can try Driving the Peg Home on a Willys. It is 51.25 inches tall to the top of its steering wheel, making the hood about 45 inches off the ground, with a flat square grill and a robust front fender. The woman may choose to anchor herself by holding on to the two all-purpose metal brackets (called "hardpoints"), which are located near the headlights.

In the Trunk

⚠ Precautions: Make sure there is a reasonable oxygen supply (and even then, do not stay inside for longer than 15 minutes) and that you have your cell phone with you. Agree on a code word in case either of you wants to get out. You won't have much room to maneuver, so take off as many clothes as you can before getting in. You could save trunk sex as the cherry on the cake after an evening's more athletic activity on the back seat, but take care not to fall asleep.

This carmic position was inspired by the action, or promise of it, between Jennifer Lopez and George Clooney in the 1998 film *Out of Sight*. US Marshall Karen Sisco (Lopez) is bundled into the trunk of her own Ford with irresistible bank robber Jim Foley (Clooney). Now that's *Carma Sutra* at its best!

Ford claims that their new 500 model now has a trunk capacity of 21.2 cubic feet, making it the biggest trunk in the sedan world. For comparison, the Chrysler 300 has only 15.6 cubic feet of trunk space. Trunk sex is not really suitable for sports cars, or any rear-engine model, which rules the Porsche 911 out on both counts. It's safest to stick to large, family-style sedans, all of which come with a trunk capacity of 18 to 20 cubic feet. If you own one of these, it is probably because you have kids. However, if the school run is making you forget how you ever ended up with children in the first place, trunk sex can be an intriguing way to spice up the humdrum routine of married life. So go ahead, get cozy, and indulge in some Clooney–Lopez role play.

MAJOR HAZARD All Ford, Lincoln, Mercury, and Toyota cars come with a standard emergency trunk release system. This manual, quick-pull lever glows in the dark and is designed for preschoolers who inadvertently lock themselves in. Be careful not to pull it during sex or you may reveal yourselves to passers-by. If you have an older model, check your manual before getting started and familiarize yourself with the escape procedure. Pack an extra set of keys and a mini-flashlight. If your car doesn't have a trunk-release lever, stick to in- or on-car fun.

Top cars for trunk fun >

> Ford 500 (21.2cu ft)
> Mercury Montego (21cu ft)
> Lincoln Town Car (21cu ft)
> Ford Crown Victoria (20.6cu ft)
> Lexus LS 430 (20.2cu ft)
> Cadillac DeVille (DTS) (18.8cu ft)
> Chrysler Concord (18.7cu ft)
> Dodge Intrepid (18.4cu ft)
> BMW 7-series (18cu ft)
> Pontiac Bonneville (18cu ft)

Positions >

You and your partner must be similar in height and flexibility to attempt either of these positions:
♥ **Mandarin Ducks (as shown)**
♥ The Crab Embrace

Pre-date Checklist

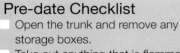

- [ ] Open the trunk and remove any storage boxes.
- [ ] Take out anything that is flammable, or that has sharp points.
- [ ] There is no need to remove the spare tire if it is fitted into a well.

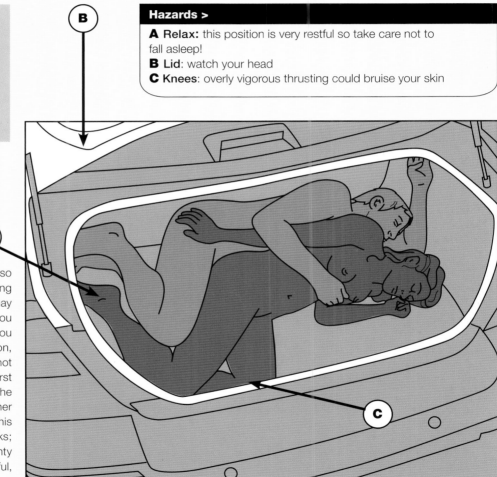

Hazards >

A Relax: this position is very restful so take care not to fall asleep!
B Lid: watch your head
C Knees: overly vigorous thrusting could bruise your skin

The Ford 500

The 500 can take eight full-size golf bags, so it will easily accommodate most consenting couples. However capacious the trunk may be, there still won't be much headroom, so you are going to have to be lying down. Unless you are both very compact, the Spoons position, with rear entry, is the most practical. It's not courteous, but the man should get in first and lie down facing outward, curving to fit the space. Then the woman gets in and fits her body into his, with her back to his chest. This position is also known as Mandarin Ducks; although you fit tightly together, there is plenty of room for the man to thrust. It is also restful, as no one has to defy gravity.

The Sedan

Precautions: Most sedans boast on-road performance combined with imposing exterior styling. Park discreetly or you may attract an audience for your carmic performance.

The Position of Equals (pictured) is a perfect fit. It's a relatively straightforward woman-on-top position that puts her in the metaphorical driver's seat. She controls speed, pace, and rhythm. Large door openings make entry into the vehicle easy, and the man must assume his position first. Make sure that the large, electronically adjustable bucket passenger seat is both fully reclined and pushed back to avoid dashed romantic hopes. Make sure the door is properly closed and locked to prevent an unplanned exit. The man takes up his position, sitting sideways in the seat with his legs apart. The woman sits astride him and leans back, gripping his ankles with her hands to help keep her steady while directing the pelvic action. This is a give-and-take position and should result in democratic delight in terms of timing and intensity of pleasure.

MAJOR HAZARD Never use the parking brake for support during the Position of Equals, or you might accidentally disengage it and make more than the earth move.

Positions >

Go for a slow, comfortable ride, such as:
- ♥ **Position of Equals (as shown)**
- ♥ Snake Trap
- ♥ The Seducer

The Chrysler 300

The Chrysler Sedan features a very spacious interior (overall, more than 106.6 cubic feet of passion room) and dimensions that most *Carma Sutra* practitioners fantasize about. Most of the useful space is in the front, where you can appreciate headroom of 38.7 inches, hiproom of 55.9 inches, and legroom of 41.8 inches. The Chrysler can seat four tall adults, so invite friends to join you if that appeals. Stylish, well-appointed, with a handcrafted feel, its comforting environment contains lashings of leather and smooth, strokable wood. Go, sweet chariot.

2.7 (A) Its ostentatious styling may attract unwanted attention; **(B)** excellent headroom for both partners; **(C)** roomy bucket seat offers bounce, comfort, and side and lumbar support.

The Hatchback

⚠ **Precautions:** Most hatchbacks are 2-door, 2-seaters—made for one plus one equals two, and some limited weekend luggage. You might think that hatchbacks are more functional than romantic, designed only to get you from A to B without many thrills, such as leather, lumbar support, DVD players, or made-for-love rear seats. But true *Carma Sutra* enthusiasts know better. There's still plenty of fun to be had in any type of car no matter how small—even in a tiny, 2-seat hatchback.

The obvious location for making out in a hatchback is the cargo area, which will be snug but still roomy enough to try out the Snake Trap (pictured), especially if you can move the seats forward. This position is perfect for tantalizing mutual enjoyment, both physical and visual. Although this position doesn't allow for deep penetration, you can consider it a way to spend quality time together.

The man assumes a sitting position and invites the woman to sit astride him, face to face, her buttocks between his upper thighs and her legs on either side of his semi-reclining body. The lovers then grip one another's feet (or ankles), leaning back at first, then enjoying the rocking motion, locking gazes for extra sexual tension or enjoying a full view of the seesaw action for added stimulation. It's a hands-on, slightly playful position, accompanied by rather limited thrusting, which makes it generally more pleasurable for the woman than the man. But if it's been a long journey, both driver and passenger might welcome the chance to just tease and play.

Top hatchbacks for carmic fun >

> VW Rabbit
> Mini Cooper
> Ford Focus
> Dodge Caliber
> Rover SD1
> Toyota Scion xB
> Honda Fit
> SAAB 9000
> Chevrolet Malibu Maxx
> Audi A3
> Chrysler

MAJOR HAZARD This position can be quite physically demanding in the confines of a hatchback, so you will need to do back and stomach muscle-strengthening exercises for it to be sustainable and enjoyable. See page 73 for our mind, body, and spirit exercises. If the pain outweighs the pleasure, there are plenty of ways to have fun in the front seat (*see pages 24–25*).

The Honda Insight

The Honda Insight boasts 47.4 cubic feet of interior volume in all, as well as a fully carpeted floor space, rear window defroster, and a rather futuristic-looking digital instrument cluster that tells you all about the Integrated Motor Assist System. But you don't need to know about these features to enjoy the position of choice for this intimate vehicle, the Snake Trap—also known as the Forming of the H Logo.

2.8 (A) Form the H logo in the snug cargo area, heightening brand and sexual awareness, **(B)** but remember headroom is limited.

The Convertible

⚠ **Precautions: The small convertible is a vehicle made for two. Don't even think about inviting a third party to join you for the ride—there simply isn't the room for a *ménage à trois* or more—so keep it between yourselves.**

The Suspended Congress (pictured) has a steep learning curve for some, and you might get more attention than you bargained for. Park somewhere private and apply high-factor sunscreen to avoid unwanted burns on sunny days. Make sure the roof is lowered in advance: you don't want to be struggling with the removal of too many tops at once. This position demands a high level of skill and agility, and should not be attempted in darkness. The man stands upright on the seat, knees slightly bent, pressing them against the comfortable, but supportive, ultra-high-tensile steel seats that minimize unwanted vertical movement and supply vital rigidity. The woman places her arms around his neck, and he supports her by the thighs or by the buttocks, depending on preference. She clasps either side of his waist with her thighs and Suspended Congress can begin.

Pre-date Checklist

- You are strongly advised to choose the black cloth-trimmed upholstery over the more slippery, and expensive, leather alternative.
- Keep valuables safe in the lockable central compartment—passers-by might help themselves to your possessions and catch you *in flagrante*.
- Avoid using the 7-speaker sound system during congress or you may attract an unwanted audience.

Top cars for top-down fun >

Pop the top on these ten popular convertibles:
- > Ford Mustang
- > Chevrolet Corvette
- > Pontiac Solstice
- > Saturn Sky
- > Nissan 350Z Roadster
- > Ferrari F430 Spider
- > Mini Cooper Convertible
- > Porsche 911 Cabriolet
- > **Mazda MX-5 Miata (as shown)**
- > Mercedes-Benz SLK

The Mazda MX-5 Miata

This is the perfect vehicle for some top-down, open-air thrills. Inject fresh oxygen into those parts of your romantic life that have lain dormant for too long. This 2-seat, rear-wheel-drive car is lithe, shiny, and quite a looker. The latest version is longer, wider, and roomier in the cockpit than previous makes, boasting 43.1 inches of front legroom (more than a whole inch more than most cars of this size). So stretch out and relax after a strenuous engagement in Suspended Congress.

2.9 Air, asphalt, action! **(A)** Ultra-high-tensile seats offer relaxation after the ride; **(B)** the man can lean against the top of the windshield if he needs a breather; **(C)** restyled headlamps and color-coordinated bumper make this one sexy automobile.

3. Advanced Driving

Now we shift gears to look at the practice of *Carma Sutra* in specific vehicles, paying particular attention to dimensions (head, leg, hip, and knee room), possible seat configurations, and accessories that can enhance or hinder your carmic ride. The principles you learned in earlier chapters are applicable to most of the vehicles that follow, but don't hesitate to experiement and create your own carmic repertoire by adding refinements and finessing your options.

We've covered all classes of vehicles, so the *Carma Sutra* can be enjoyed by everybody. For luxury lovers, there is the Rolls-Royce Phantom; for those that like to keep on the job, the Ford F-350 Super Duty. If size is your thing, try the Hummer, and if you like to take the road less traveled, the Jeep offers rugged endurance. There is the Toyota Scion for adaptable lovers, or the Prius for those who love the planet as much as they love each other. The T-Bird is for oldschool speed merchants; the Stretch Lincoln Town Car for people who like to be driven. There is even a two-wheel option: the Harley-Davidson Softail.

A specific position is recommended for each vehicle, often accompanied by a few alternative options. Every kind of position is covered—sitting, lying, kneeling, face-to-face, face-to-back, man on top, woman on top, and oral. For handy reference, gatefolds display every position suggested, demonstrated by consenting crash-test dummies.

To get the most out of this section, you can either check the entry for the vehicle you already own, or look for the positions you like and find out which car would be best to buy/rent/borrow. If you can't get your hands on the precise model, you can always improvise by using a car of the same category (sedan, wagon, SUV, convertible, coupe, hatchback, minivan, truck), studying the specs, and then adapting the carmic instructions to suit. That is what advanced driving is all about.

On Two Wheels: Harley-Davidson Softail

⚠ **Precautions:** Sex on a Softail sounds like an exotic cocktail, and, though it certainly quenches a deep thirst, it can be physically demanding as well. It's no walk in the park, not even for a Hell's Angel. You need to be agile, flexible, and endowed with an acute sense of balance, timing, and consideration. But don't worry, it is just like riding a bicycle— once you've done it, you'll never forget how.

No ride is ever lonely on a Harley, according to the advertising guys. For some hog owners their passions are stoked more by their bikes than their partners. This comes as no surprise, given all those shiny chrome features, deeply padded leather seats, and sensuous, rounded curves, in colors such as black cherry, brandy wine sunglow, and deep cobalt pearl. However, male bikers should remember that when practicing the *Carma Sutra* on a Harley Softail, the only thing between them and their mount is a beautiful, supine woman. What better union, what mightier *ménage à trois*, what more perfect choice than the Yawning Position (pictured)?

According to traditional sutras, this pose is often adopted spontaneously by lovers— perfect for Harley guys. The woman positions herself carefully on the low, wide, and deeply padded saddle, her back supported by the 1450cc 88B Blockhead engine. She raises her thighs and parts her legs widely to accommodate her man, who straddles the pillion seat and leans forward. Partners can clasp fingers for extra poise and intimacy.

MAJOR HAZARD Cramped muscles are a concern during this position. Prepare your body with yoga or Pilates, and by stretching. The Yawning Position requires the man to be kneeling, but for carmic purposes he should support himself with one leg on the ground.

Tips >

> First things first: park the bike safely and securely. Remember, it is going to see some serious engines-off action.
> The woman is in a precarious position, although she can clutch the man's sides for balance.

Positions >

You can't be overly ambitious on two wheels—remember the Hog can only be parked on its kickstand—so choose a position that will ensure a stable ride.
♥ Encircling Position
♥ **Yawning Position (as shown)**
♥ Sporting of the Swan

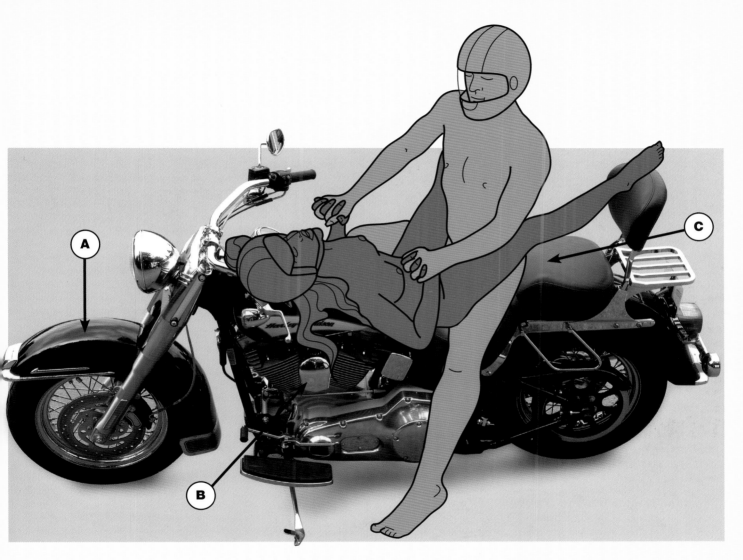

3.1 (A) Check out your reflection in the seductive black paintwork; **(B)** Blockhead engine provides support for the woman; **(C)** deeply padded seat offers comfort for the man.

Classic Cruiser: Dodge Dart

⚠️ **Precautions:** Your Dodge Dart will have some serious mileage under its fan belt, and unless you have been automanic about preserving its enduring good looks and smooth running engine (*see* Essential Maintenance, *pages 72–3*), it may not appear to be a very inviting venue for *Carma Sutra* action. But there's more here than meets the eye.

It may have been a hit in '63, but it's no little deuce coupe. The Dodge Dart was made for durability and longevity, and the 2-door model sports a compact yet spacious design. Its 111-inch wheelbase supports a generous interior and delivers more room for maneuvering than you might imagine. This is further enhanced by retracting the roof, which comes complete with plastic windows, allowing you to enjoy a topless ride with panoramic views.

The Encircling Position (pictured) is an appropriately open and enjoyable one. The woman lies on her back across the rear bench. She then lifts her feet, crossing her calves. The man follows her into the rear seat, positioning himself between her buttocks, leaning over her during congress. He supports himself with his arms during what is a stimulating, open-to-the-elements experience.

MAJOR HAZARD There was a whole lot of lovin' in the '60s so your Dodge Dart Convertible will have seen quite a bit of action during that period, if not since. Be sure the chassis is up to some more. And if you are as rusty as your vehicle, you might want to take a test ride first.

Tips >

> Try to clean or smarten up your Dodge as much as you can, or consider spicing things up by using a blindfold.

> If your model has its original '60s Naugahyde® plastic, it may not be in pristine condition; supplying a throw will make it more inviting, and a pillow for the woman's head is a nice touch.

Positions >

There's enough room in a Dodge for various sitting and kneeling positions.
♥ Lotus Position
♥ **Encircling Position (as shown)**
♥ White Tiger
♥ Raised Feet Posture
♥ Position of Equals

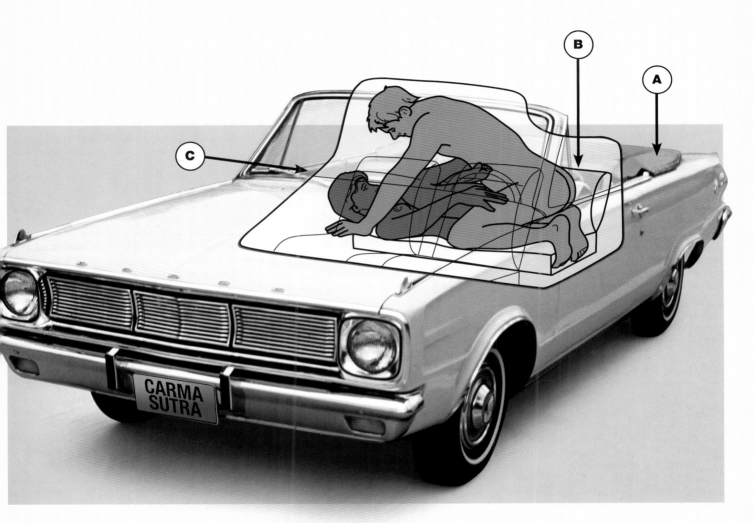

3.2 (A) Retracting roof offers room for maneuvering; **(B)** spacious interior with plenty of trunk space; **(C)** watch out for the some of the interior trim, which can be rough on naked, impassioned bodies.

4 x 4 Play: **Toyota FJ Cruiser**

⚠ **Precautions:** The 2007 Toyota FJ Cruiser is the Big Daddy of SUVs, not a Soccer Mom vehicle. It's for young male bucks (with about 20,000 of them in their wallet).

The new Toyota FJ cruiser is retro-futuristic in design, complete with wrapround rear glass. The perfect *Carma Sutra* position to complement its "wilderness tamed" mantra: the Sporting of the Swan. Use the reverse-opening rear door to gain access to the roomy cargo area, and fold down the rear seats to create a long, flat surface generous enough to accommodate this ambitious pose. The position allows the male to recline full-length in the spacious, if utilitarian, interior. The very ample headroom of 40.3 inches allows the woman to sit astride her partner, her back to him, tucking her feet next to, or even under, his upper thighs to anchor herself. She lowers herself onto him, grips both his knees and thereby controls the depth, pace, and vigor of the action, while the man enjoys an action-packed rear view.

MAJOR HAZARD This is a relatively advanced position and must be executed with a degree of care. The woman should not be tempted to lean too far forward. Take it easy—you don't want to have to call a carma mechanic.

Pre-date Checklist

☐ While the cargo area offers 66 cubic feet of space, its interior is spartan and has nothing in the way of soft furnishings. You might want to bring a camping mattress for extra comfort and to prevent injury.

Positions >

Ample space in the cargo area creates opportunities for reclining positions.
- ♥ Transverse Lute
- ♥ **Sporting of the Swan (as shown)**
- ♥ Reverse Cowgirl

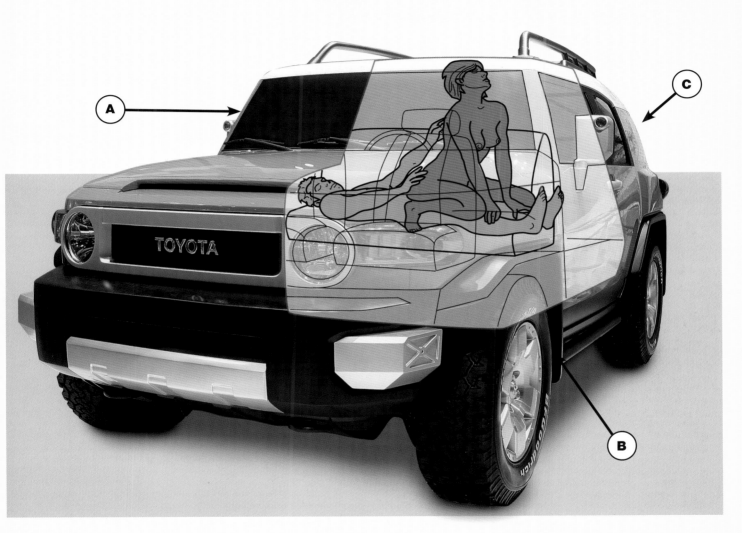

3.3 (A) Tinted glass for extra privacy; **(B)** tough off-road suspension handles the bounce; **(C)** large rear doors offer a panoramic view.

Pick-up Lines: Ford F-350 Super Duty

Precautions: This is the ultimate heavy-duty pickup truck. However, only very advanced *Carma Sutra* followers should perform the position of choice in the bed of the truck without practicing it in the safety of the cab first.

This vehicle is for the working man, for whom large loads hold no fear. With its 362 HP Ford Triton® V10 gasoline engine, able to churn out 457 lb.-ft. of torque, the Super Duty is designed for hauling and towing, tackling uneven terrain, and delivering smooth rides over the bumpiest of surfaces. It is the perfect lifestyle choice for macho, muscular males, who, as Ford themselves put it, want to conquer, rule, triumph, and command.

No question as to which is the ideal *Carma Sutra* position for this working man's tool: it has to be the Fixing of a Nail Position (pictured). During this symbolic yet practical pose, the woman slides onto the roomy back bench and lies down, while her partner assumes his position on top. She stretches one leg out flat but bends the other back as far as possible, placing her heel on her man's forehead, a pose made possible by the 41.1 inches of headroom. If you opt for front-seat fixing, fold down the center arm first to avoid unscheduled DIY—and remember, should any equipment need fixing, you can always reach for the handy built-in tool kit.

MAJOR HAZARD The Fixing of a Nail is a precision position, not one for amateurs. It requires agility, flexibility, and a certain level of fitness. The woman can use the door handle for support, and the man has roof ride handles to grip for really bumpy rides.

Tips >

> Try out your performance in the roomy, fully boxed cab section first, making full use of the 40/20/40 split bench front seat or the FlexFold™ 60/40 split bench with outboard head restraint (available on the Lariat model).

Positions >

The king-size F-350 (particularly the truck's bed) offers you plenty of options—sitting, standing, and reclining:
- ❤ Pair of Tongs
- ❤ Suspended Congress
- ❤ **Fixing of a Nail (as shown)**
- ❤ Pounding on the Spot

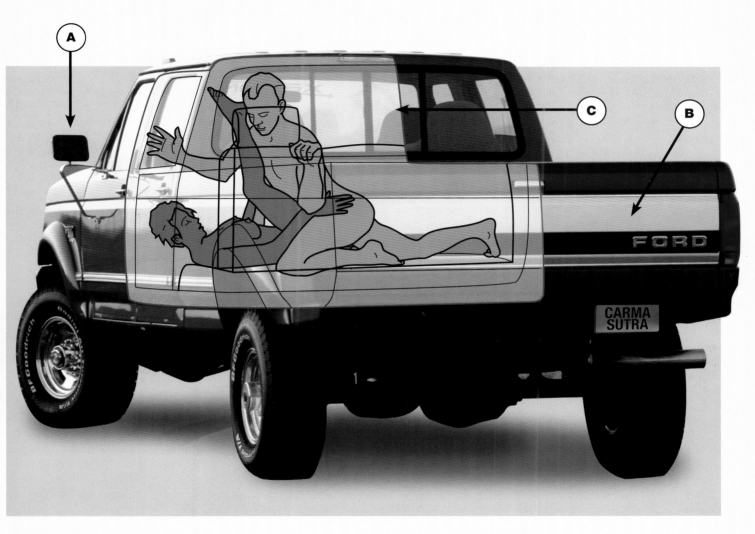

3.4 (A) Check your profile in the extended mirrors; **(B)** for roadside repairs, there's a built-in tool kit at your disposal; **(C)** slide-open rear windows for ventilation.

Environmental Sex: Toyota Prius Mk II

⚠️ **Precautions: The Prius starts with its electric engine then switches to gas, either for more speed or to recharge the battery. Be sure the car really has stopped before you begin—the engine purrs so quietly, you may not notice that it's still switched on.**

The Prius is powered by a Hybrid Synergy Drive. It has an electric and a gasoline engine, and an onboard computer that regulates them, keeping carbon emissions to a minimum and designating it as a SULEV (Super Ultra Low-Emission Vehicle) and PZEV (Partial Zero Emissions Vehicle). For carmic fun, the Mk II is a better choice than the Mk I, being roomier, especially in the back.

The gears are controlled by a tiny joystick on the dashboard (you select, the computer does the rest). You can also adjust the height and angle of the console that separates the front bucket seats. Hand grips above each door will allow you to try out the driver's-seat positions suggested on page 24. If things get hot, run the air-conditioning by pressing the ignition button to activate the electric engine (see Major Hazard box below).

The Prius is only 67.9 inches wide so using the split back seat (which can be configured as a bench) will not be comfortable if one of you is 6 feet plus. However, you can fold down the seats to provide access to a 16-cubic-foot carpeted cargo area, which you can access via the hatchback door. Headroom is still restricted, and the cargo area is shallow (the battery that powers the electric engine is located under the trunk floor). However, the extra space scooped out of the bodywork above the rear wheel arches gives extra side-to-side space. This makes it ideal for Butterflies in Flight, a position eminently suitable for a car with the environmental credentials of the Prius. The man lies down on his back, head toward the rear, feet resting on the folded-down back seat (or the transmission block if he is tall). The woman lies on top, placing her feet on his and pushing against them to move herself up and down. They hold hands and stretch their arms out, flapping gently like butterflies, making as little impact on the environment as possible.

MAJOR HAZARD The push-button ignition system on the dash turns on the electric engine, which is noiseless. If you are engaged in driver's-seat congress with the gear in Drive and your foot falls inadvertently on the gas pedal, you could be gliding along in silent running mode before you know it. If you've chosen the iTech option, you don't even have to insert your "keyless" card into the slot; just have it on your person and the computer does the rest.

Tip >

> Carpooling is recommended to help cut down on pollution. You might consider offering to share your Prius with another like-minded couple, so that you can use the cargo area and the front seats at the same time.

Top environmental cars >

> Honda Insight
> Chevrolet Silverado Hybrid
> Toyota Camry Hybrid
> Lexus GS450h
> Ford Escape Hybrid
> GMC Sierra Hybrid
> Lexus RX400h
> Mercury Mariner Hybrid
> GM EV1
> Honda Civic Hybrid

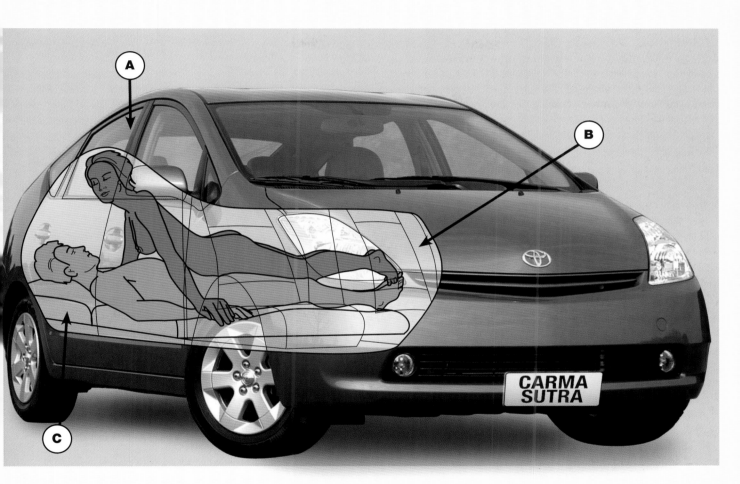

3.5 (A) Restricted headroom, especially in the back; **(B)** but still offers 38.6 inches of legroom and 51 inches of hiproom; **(C)** battery located below cargo area favors supine carmic options.

A Tight Squeeze: Kia Rio

⚠ **Precautions:** The Kia Rio makes no false claims about size, capacity, or comfort and requires you to do the same. Its dimensions speak for themselves. Available as sedan or a wagon, the Kia Rio is compact, especially in the front, and unsuitable for extravagant *Carma Sutra* positions, unusually tall or heavy lovers, or threesomes.

The Rio's bucket front seats are not ideally suited to romance, but passion can still bloom in a small greenhouse, making it the perfect environment for the Lotus position. In order for the couple to fit in the vehicle, the man needs to be cross-legged. Sharing the passenger seat is going to demand a level of suppleness that only the most flexible lovers possess.

The man gets comfortable first, and once he is safely ensconced with his legs crossed, the woman lowers herself onto him and neatly draws up her crossed legs behind his back, in an unfolding, lotus-like pose. The man clasps her in his arms, while she holds the height-adjustable headrests to guide and control her movement. Let's hope you went for the optional air-conditioning if things get really heated (although some reports indicate that overuse of the A/C leads to a sluggish engine when the car is restarted; no good if you want a quick getaway). Fixed cup holders in the map pockets can be used for storing refreshments.

MAJOR HAZARD The Rio's unique selling point is its low cost, and on early models money was saved on the interior trim, a sea of plastic. Also, severe post-coital cramping is possible in this vehicle. Stretching before and after congress is recommended.

Tip >

> Don't deploy the driver's seat fold-down armrest; it impedes already limited arm movement. And avoid leaning on the big rectangular hazard button.

Positions >

♥ **Lotus Position (as shown)**
There is more room for experimentation in the back. Consider:
♥ Crab Embrace
♥ Raised Feet

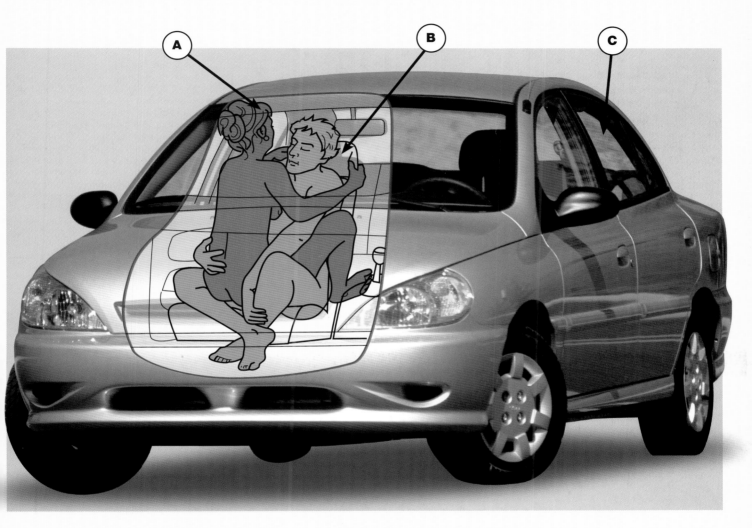

3.6 (A) Restricted head- and legroom means the Lotus position is the ideal choice; **(B)** adjustable headrests provide stability; **(C)** small windows for discretion.

Off-Road Activity: Jeep Wrangler

⚠ **Precautions: This is a go-anywhere vehicle made for off-road activity and all that comes with it. Its interior is spartan yet functional, so if your parts are more baby soft than Lara Croft, stick to less-rugged vehicles.**

The Jeep Wrangler is sturdy, built for bump- and hump-handling and all-terrain affairs. The 2007 version boasts new, improved rear-seat legroom of 37.2 inches, but it remains a utilitarian vehicle. Whichever model you have, choose the rear as the location for love and the Reverse Cowgirl (pictured) as your position (best achieved with the roof off). It is still quite a big step up into the Jeep, and the man should clamber in first.

Once safely ensconced in the rear, the man can take full advantage of the 60/40 split seat by folding it flat and reclining upon it in readiness (if you've got an older version you can still achieve this position by pushing the seats back). The woman then positions herself on top, facing toward the front, his legs between hers. The woman controls angle, depth, and pace while the man reclines, stimulates his partner (optional), and generally enjoys both the ride and the view. If things get rough, the seat-mounted supplemental side airbags will soften the blow. Play your favorite off-roading music on the 50-watt sub-woofer hidden in the central console. And be sure to load up on sunscreen before you head to the hills.

| **MAJOR HAZARD** | The 2007 model has a 3-piece modular hard roof or Sunrider soft top. If you choose to go topless, check the weather report before heading out. A sudden thunderstorm could dampen your ardor considerably. |

Positions >

This is a get-up-and-go vehicle that demands some rocking good positions:
- ♥ Pounding on the Spot
- ♥ **Reverse Cowgirl (as shown)**
- ♥ Butterflies in Flight

Tip>

> The Reverse Cowgirl position is the obvious modern *Carma Sutra* position for Wrangler riders, who like horsepower without the horse.

3.7 (A) Built-in rollbars can be used to supplement balance; **(B)** 40.3 inches of rear headroom with the top on; **(C)** suspension for all terrains, all activities, so hit the trail!

Truckin': Chevy Colorado Extended Cab

⚠ **Precautions:** The Chevy is a compact pickup truck with its focus on function rather than form. If your girl is more the reverse, you probably need to think twice about asking Miss American Pie to join you in the back seat of this particular vehicle.

The Chevrolet Colorado was designed for long hauls, not lengthy loving. Its interior boasts an impressive instrument panel and ample below-seat storage, but be prepared for a tight squeeze when you fold down the forward-facing rear bench to create a flat floor, normally reserved for loading purposes. Choose an intimate, skin-on-skin *Carma Sutra* pose, such as the Side-by-Side Clasping Position (pictured). If you and your squeeze weren't that close before, you certainly will be during and after this up-close-and-personal, face-to-face position.

Both partners stretch out along the seat, facing each other with legs outstretched. The woman brings her top leg between the man's and he wraps his legs around hers. Limbs are intertwined as much as possible to ensure maximum skin contact. Penetration is not very deep in this position and movement is somewhat restricted, but the aim is to enjoy a really intimate embrace rather than embark upon sustained lovemaking. Space is limited, so go steady, enjoy the clasp, and the solid rear axle suspension will do the rest.

MAJOR HAZARD Even though the cab is the extended version, you might want to keep the door open for additional room. Beware rolling into the rear leg space—you may get stuck there. Finally, refrain from making any jokes about getting Chevro-laid.

Pre-date Checklist
☐ The Chevy is made for trucking, so by all means pack a picnic—or at least a blanket.

Positions >
If you are tight on time and room, try:
♥ Transverse Lute
♥ **Side-by-Side Clasping Position (as shown)**
♥ Mandarin Ducks

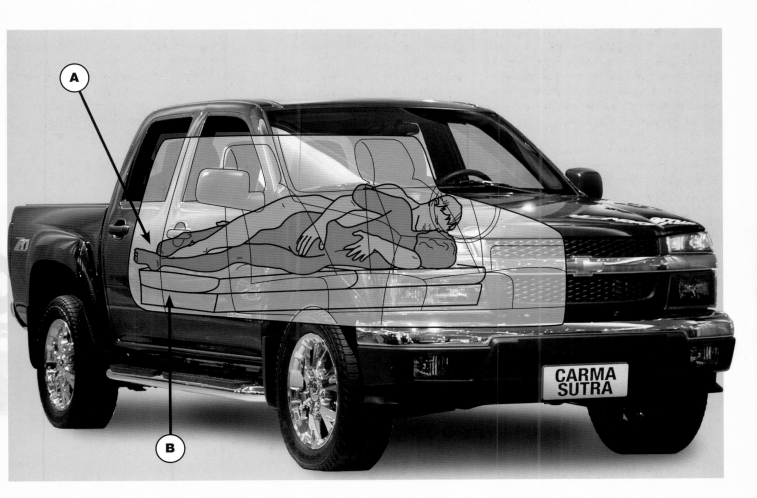

3.8 (A) Ample below-seat storage, in case this becomes a regular date; **(B)** fold-down rear seats offer a flat surface.

A Quickie: Ford GT

⚠️ **Precautions:** The Ford GT is not just another car. Potential carmic Casanovas will need to assert themselves inside its impressive, cockpit-style interior or they will end up being outclassed by their surroundings.

Back in '66 the original GT40s chewed up and spat out the Le Mans checkered flag. This 21st-century mid-engine 2-seater sports car looks back to its origins and forward to its future. Door cutouts extend into the roof to allow for smoother entry and exit. Remote keyless entry makes access even easier. The smart, leather-clad, ventilated bucket seats, complete with metal eyelets, not only keep you cool but are very low slung. So prepare for a low down experience on the firm, well-bolstered seats. You may want to put a supportive cushion over the console for extra comfort, and drape soft cashmere over the aluminum rings to avoid an unattractive skin dimpling.

If cars were people, then the Ford GT would be Casanova. That's why this car is made for the best-named *Carma Sutra* position: The Seducer (pictured). Just think how the original Casanova would have delighted in this role, had he owned a GT.

The woman lies on her back across the passenger seat, making herself comfortable over the console and taking care to avoid the gearshift knob, the leather-wrapped steering wheel with tilt and telescoping, and the various aerospace-themed toggle switches that could cause discomfort. The man slides into position between her legs, supporting her buttocks with his thighs as she wraps her legs around his waist or over his shoulders, depending on size, agility, and sense of adventure. She pulls her partner toward her, locking her feet behind his waist or balancing them on his shoulders. His hands are free to support, stroke, or stimulate her upper torso. Casanova would be right at home.

MAJOR HAZARD You can take full advantage of the surprisingly generous dimensions: 44.6 inches of legroom, 57.7 inches of shoulder space, and 35.4 inches of headroom. But if you have a wide frame, things will get a bit tight, so be sure to stretch beforehand to avoid a pulled muscle.

Tips >

> Leave a door open and the roof cut out for extra headroom.
> Turn off the engine, otherwise you could be distracted by the whirring of the supercharger belt, just behind the rear window.

Positions >

Making out in the Ford GT should be an auto-erotic ride to remember.
- ♥ **The Seducer (as shown)**
- ♥ Encircling Position
- ♥ Yawning Position

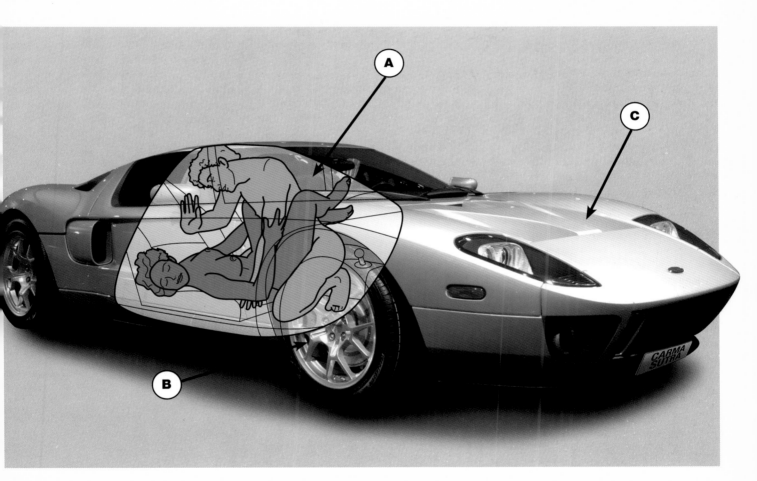

3.9 (A) Black leather-wrapped interior adds a frisson; **(B)** fully independent suspension for a smooth ride, **(C)** but there's no room for a spare, so be sure not to get a flat on the way home.

Crash Test Carma Sutra

At-a-glance guide to positions recommended for *Carma Sutra*

Man on Top
> Rising Position *(page 15)*
> Raised Feet *(page 19)*
> Crab Embrace *(gatefold 1)*
> Turning Position *(gatefold 1)*
> Variant Yawning *(gatefold 1)*
> Yawning Position *(page 39)*
> Encircling Position *(page 43)*
> Fixing of a Nail *(page 41)*
> Seducer *(page 55)*

Woman on Top
> Goat on the Tree *(page 24)*
> Sporting of the Swan *(page 43)*
> Reverse Cowgirl *(page 51)*
> Seducer *(page 55)*
> Pair of Tongs *(page 63)*

Standing
> Driving the Peg Home *(page 27)*
> Suspended Congress *(page 35)*

Kneeling
> Rising Position *(page 15)*
> White Tiger *(gatefold 1)*
> Sporting of the Swan *(page 43)*
> Tail of the Ostrich *(gatefold 2)*
> Rainbow Arch *(gatefold 2)*

Sitting
> Goat on the Tree *(page 24)*
> Position of Equals *(page 31)*
> Snake Trap *(page 33)*
> Lotus Position *(page 49)*
> Auparishtaka *(page 61)*
> Swing *(page 65)*
> Carma's Wheel *(page 68)*

Lying
> Transverse Lute *(page 13)*
> Crab Embrace *(gatefold 1)*
> Mandarin Ducks *(page 29)*
> Butterflies in Flight *(page 47)*
> Side-by-Side Clasping Position *(page 53)*
> Congress of a Crow *(page 59)*
> Fifth Posture *(page 67)*
> Rainbow Arch *(gatefold 2)*
> Cicada on a Bough *(page 69)*

Rear Entry
> Mandarin Ducks *(page 29)*
> White Tiger *(gatefold 1)*
> Sporting of the Swan *(page 43)*
> Reverse Cowgirl *(page 51)*
> Swing *(page 65)*
> Cicada on a Bough *(page 69)*

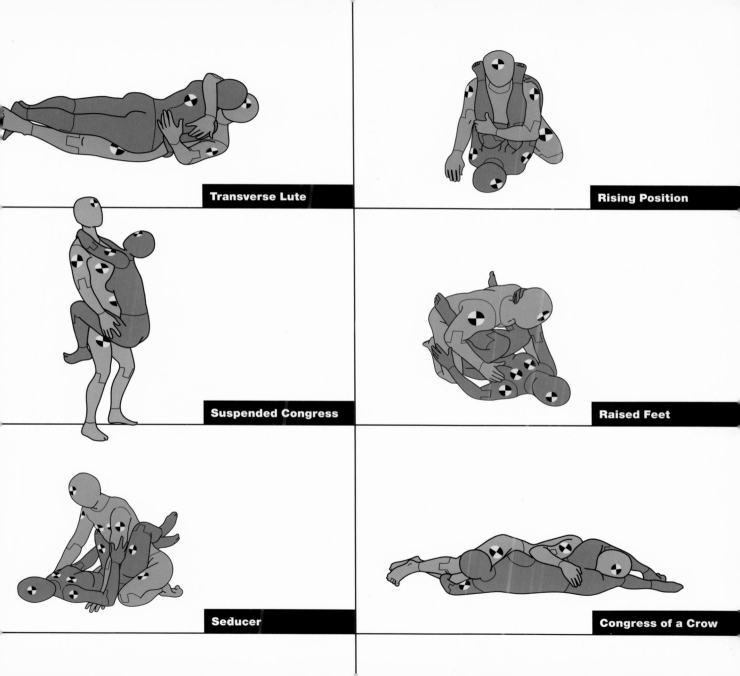

Transverse Lute

Rising Position

Suspended Congress

Raised Feet

Seducer

Congress of a Crow

3.10 (A) The very height and width of luxury; **(B)** tinted windows ensure privacy. **(C)** A mirrored ceiling, a

Extended Pleasure: Stretch Limo

⚠ **Precautions: After giving the driver instructions, close off the dividing panel and switch off the intercom. If you are easily distracted, don't activate the onboard flatscreen media centers.**

Stretch limousines come in various sizes, with room for 8 to 12 people, but a good choice would be the 5-door version that is 120 inches wide and 28 feet long. It can seat up to 10, if you're feeling particularly uninhibited. While being driven by a professional with all windows tinted, you can do what you like without having to bring the vehicle to a halt. Take advantage of the space, the soft 6-foot-long bench seats, and the wall-to-wall carpeting to try some more exotic positions. Some models have a moon/sunroof, others have mirrored ceilings or reflective Star Gazer panels featuring fiber-optic lights that dance like stars. The cabin is soundproof, and you can control the climate and mood lighting. Everything is close at hand, including ice machines (ice is great for carpet burn) and a chute for tissues and trash.

Try the Tail of the Ostrich (pictured, center), ideal if your limo has the moon/sunroof option. The woman lies along on the floor positioned under the roof, and the man kneels at her feet. He raises her legs so that they rest one on each of his shoulders, and she lifts her body so that only her shoulders and head remain on the floor. This gives the man the ideal entry position, and affords her a view of the stars above.

MAJOR HAZARD All limos come with a fully equipped bar; the glassware is securely anchored but be careful not to lash out in the throes of carmic passion, breaking glasses or bottles. Nothing ruins the moment like having to pick tiny shards of glass out of the carpet, seats, and each other, while the driver tacks $50 onto your bill.

Tips >

> Check the seat configuration to see if it fits with what you have in mind. Some have separate bench seats facing front, back, and running along the side and some have a continuous L-shaped bench.

> Devise a route that will give you maximum time for carmic activity and instruct your driver not to hurry.

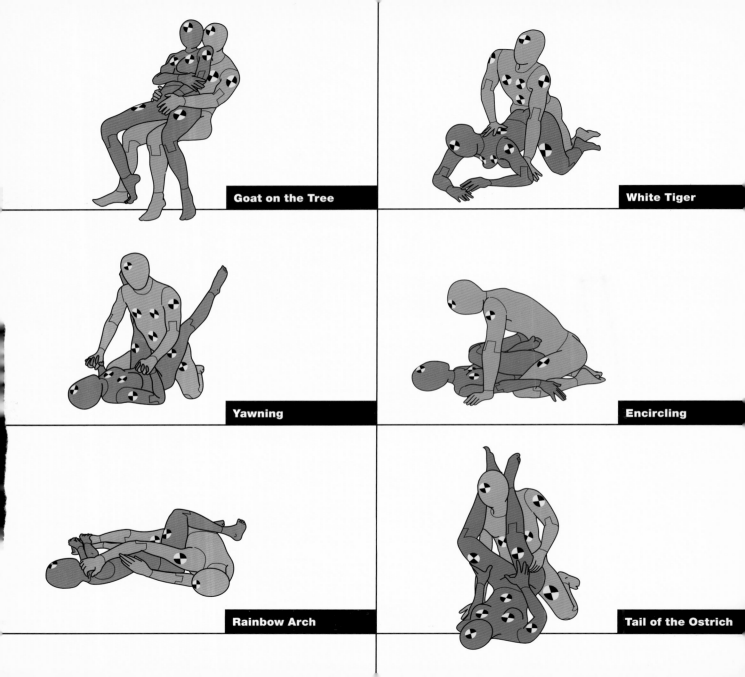

Goat on the Tree

White Tiger

Yawning

Encircling

Rainbow Arch

Tail of the Ostrich

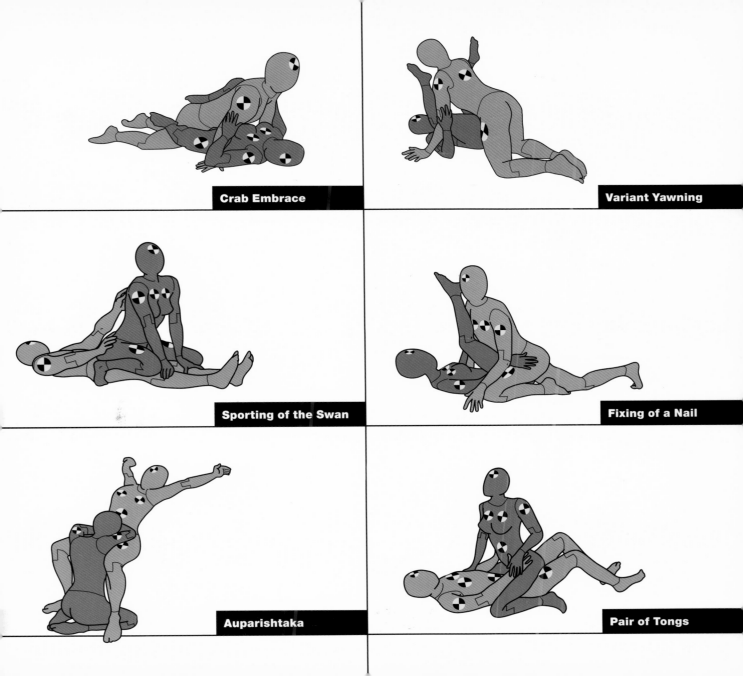

Crab Embrace

Variant Yawning

Sporting of the Swan

Fixing of a Nail

Auparishtaka

Pair of Tongs

Extended Pleasure (cont)

All that floor space comes into its own for side-by-side positions. Try the Rainbow Arch (pictured, far left)—you may not be able to maintain it for long, but incorporating it into an extended lovemaking session can be fun. This unusual entwining position is especially good for the woman. She lies on her side, one leg raised, and her partner lies between her legs, facing the other way. She grasps his legs or feet while he grips her shoulders or holds her upper back.

If there are more than two of you (and a stretch limo can accommodate at least three couples) use the back bench for seated positions, such as the Position of Equals (pictured, right—*see also pages 30–31*). Use the long side bench for relaxing, stretched-out face-to-face positions; straightforward missionary positions; or the Elephant Posture, in which the woman lies face down, her legs slightly parted, and the man lies on top of her with his legs between hers, supporting himself on his hands or forearms. The original *Kama Sutra* discusses the Congress of a Herd of Elephants, which is the same position but with one man and several women. Consider this optional.

Stretch cars for extensive fun >

> Lincoln Town Car Limousine
> Cadillac DTS
> Chrysler 300C
> Hummer H2
> Cadillac Escalade

Positions >

There are no limits in a long limo. Try:
♥ **Rainbow Arch (as shown)**
♥ **Tail of the Ostrich (as shown)**
♥ **Position of Equals (as shown)**
♥ Elephant Posture
♥ Congress of a Crow

Tip >

> For a faster thrill, ask your driver to choose roads with some sharp bends or at least an incline or two.

to-wall carpeting offer options for the adventurous. **(E)** A fully-equipped bar for post-carmic refreshment.

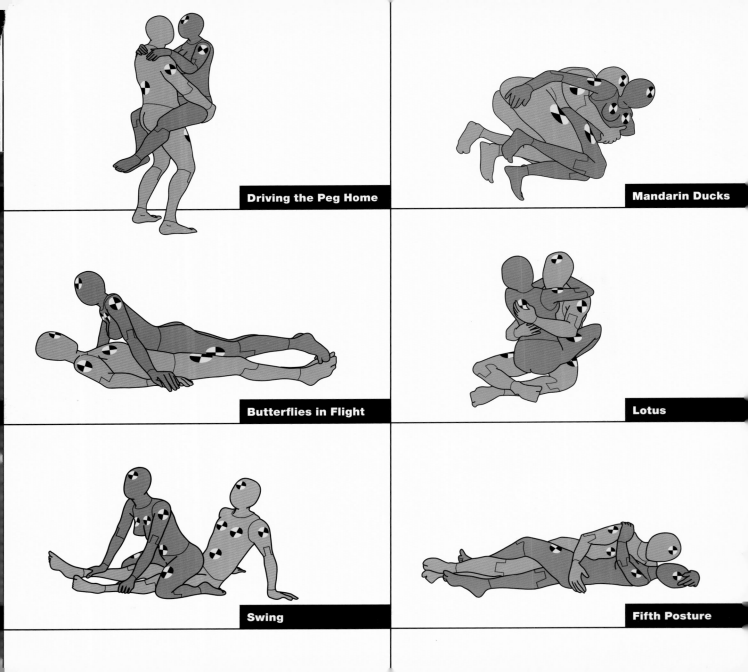

Driving the Peg Home

Mandarin Ducks

Butterflies in Flight

Lotus

Swing

Fifth Posture

Position of Equals

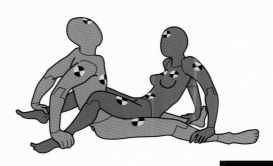

SnakeTrap

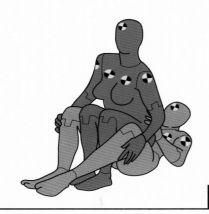

Reverse Cowgirl

Side-by-Side Clasping position

Cicada on a Bough

Executive Toy: Rolls-Royce Phantom

⚠ **Precautions: A Phantom engages all the senses. It feels good, looks good, smells good—even sounds good, with its reassuringly silent doors. If money is no object then this is the car for you. Otherwise, stick to a sedan that costs less than $300,000.**

With its iconic Spirit of Ecstasy hood ornament (which, by the way, can be lowered at the touch of a button), the Phantom symbolizes, even craves, luxurious, private, intimate indulgence. You won't be able to stop yourself from admiring its perfect details and caressing its walnut interior before you sink into the wide, yawning expanse of the rear seat with its 56.3 inches of shoulder room and 38.5 inches of headroom. In the back is where all the best people sit, after all, and where Congress of a Crow (pictured) can be enjoyed in the quintessential lap of luxury. With its specially curved sides and supple, foldaway armrest, the leather-upholstered seat with superb finishing is the perfect place for a profoundly intimate, sensual, and mutually satisfying position.

The man allows the woman to enter the car first, as etiquette demands, then he slides carefully in beside her, using the opposite door, so that simultaneous oral pleasuring can begin. The reverse-opening doors close at the touch of a button, and almost noiselessly, so proceedings are barely interrupted and the moment not lost. The man pleasures the woman orally while stimulating other parts of her body with his hands. The woman utilizes various mouth techniques, thereby maximizing her partner's auto-erotic pleasure.

You might consider customizing your vehicle by adding a wet bar to the central console for post-coital refreshments. Handcrafted folding picnic tables are available for that revitalizing post-congress snack.

Positions >

For a luxurious experience, try any of the lying positions, such as:
- ♥ **Congress of a Crow (as shown)**
- ♥ Transverse Lute

MAJOR HAZARD

Real leather seats can be slippery, so you might want to invest in a pure cashmere throw to prevent disruption or injury, and for protective purposes. A Rolls-Royce will attract attention wherever it is parked, so beware of curious onlookers (unless you've parked on your private estate, of course).

Tips >

> You may want to dispense with the services of a chauffeur.
> A small rear window will ensure discretion throughout the "inverted congress."
> Consider curtains, should you require total privacy.

3.11 (A) Enjoy the leather seating and **(B)** walnut detailing; **(C)** opt for the extended wheelbase version to maximize the shag-carpeted floorspace in the back.

Military Maneuvers: Hummer H2

⚠ **Precautions: The Hummer is a big car, built for those whose DNA (driver's natural attributes) includes ruggedness (personal and geographic), resourcefulness, and a love of tackling tough terrain. It is a statement vehicle. If your car speaks louder than your actions, choose something more subtle.**

The Hummer H2 commands the highway and the unmade track, but it gained real street cred, thanks to Arnie Schwarzenegger, by combining robust practicality with a roomy, luxurious interior for those who prefer to stick to the city. The H2 gives men pleasure at the wheel, but they can enjoy the ride as much—if not more—during the Auparishtaka pose (pictured), while comfortably stretched out in the electronically-controlled, 8-way power bucket passenger seat, with its 4-way lumbar adjustments, plus tilt facility and built-in preferred position memory. The all-terrain alpha male enters the vehicle first, through wide-opening doors that make entry and exit a breeze, then sinks into a semi-reclining position in the passenger seat and makes full use of the generous amount of shoulder room and long, wide cushions.

For full pleasure, he should tilt and push back as far as possible before his partner assumes her kneeling pose, made comfortable by no fewer than 62 inches of legroom. She can then pleasure her partner with the eponymous humming technique to create good vibrations. Dual zone front-seat climate controls allow driver and passenger to specify their preferred temperatures—up to 25 degrees in difference—which will ensure mutual comfort. The man should be careful in the throes of passion since this could cause extreme discomfort for him and his lover.

In the summer months, couples can enjoy the excellent circulation provided by the HVAC system and the comfort of heat-reflective glass. Tinted glass on the cabin and rear ensure privacy during this intimate act. Deep map pockets running the entire length of the front and rear doors allow for storage of marital aids.

MAJOR HAZARD The woman can practice the hummer technique with the rhythms from selected tracks played on the MP3 X-player and integrated 9-speaker stereo sound system. However, hardcore rap is not recommended during the Auparishtaka pose.

Tips >

> In winter, switch on the heated front seat well in advance to ensure everything's warmed up and ready for carmic action.
> The rubber or carpet floor mats can be a little harsh on the woman's knees during the Auparishtaka pose, so pack a cushion for comfort.

Positions >

The interior of the H2 is spacious and comfortable so choices are limitless. Try:
♥ **Auparishtaka (as shown)**
♥ Snake Trap
♥ Raised Feet
♥ Sporting of the Swan

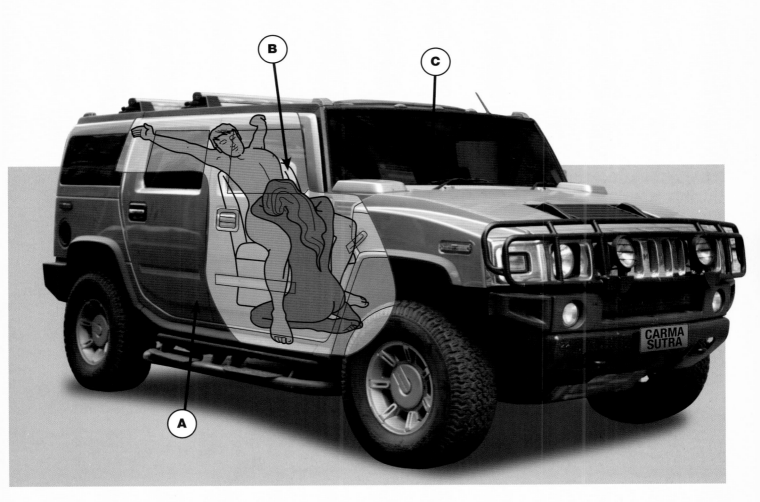

3.12 (A) Wide-opening doors for smooth entry and exit; **(B)** heated seatbacks and cushions come standard; **(C)** dual front-seat controls enable carmic couples to set individual temperatures for comfort.

Rock 'n' Roll: '55 Thunderbird

⚠ **Precautions:** There's every reason to do a song and dance about the '55 T-Bird. It is an enduring symbol of youth and passion, and was built for fun, fun, fun. It heralded the arrival of a new forward-looking era, so if you aren't an optimistic soul, this isn't the car for you. Stick to a family sedan.

The '55 Thunderbird is an iconic two-seat roadster, deriving its name from a Native American god of desert rain. It's a feel-good, drive-in-movie car, and only an enjoyable, iconic, stylish *Carma Sutra* position befits it. An appropriate choice for the Torch Red T-Bird is the Pair of Tongs, also known as the Naturally

Inverted T (pictured). For this, the man lies on his back across the red-and-white front bench, his head on the passenger side, his legs slightly bent if the doors are closed or extended if the open. The woman sits astride her partner, her legs bent at the knee. The woman then draws him into her, alternating between subtle and slightly more forceful pressure, accompanied by smooth pelvic movements. Partners can hold hands during lovemaking, enhancing both intimacy and pleasure.

MAJOR HAZARD Ensure that neither underbody nor frame are damaged by rust before engaging in particularly energetic positions or you may ruin your undercarriage. Remember: things were built differently in '55, and you will have to manually roll up your windows should the great T-Bird send rain during your *Carma Sutra* session.

Tips >

> Best performed after dispensing with the removable hardtop, which grants the couple greater freedom of expression and room for maneuvering during this woman-on-top, baby-let's-ride position.
> She can check for unexpected guests through the wraparound aircraft-style windshield, should she feel the need.

Position >

Carma Sutra statisticians calculate that with customized variations and add-ons, the total number of possible positions is 16,000—the exact number of '55 T-Bird models produced. However, the Naturally Inverted T really is the only acceptable position for this long-nosed, reverse-wedge vehicle.

3.13 (A) Removable hard top allows the woman plenty of room for maneuvering; **(B)** highly polished mirror chrome for self-admiration; and **(C)** 2,980 lb of V8 engine, all add up to full ego thrust.

Customizable Love: Toyota Scion xB

⚠️ **Precautions: This car is a head-turner, but more in a "what!?" than a "wow!" kind of way. Do you think outside the box? Do you value what lies inside? If you are a non-lateral, superficial person, this unusual, high-roof, 4-door, rectilinear wagon-cum-utility vehicle is not for you.**

It's not beautiful but people fall for it. The French would call the Scion xB *joli laid*, a rather apt description given its roomy suitability for *Carma Sutra* consummation, and, like some poses, it delivers more than its looks might suggest. Designed for the young, it has found fans among many young-at-heart lovers as well.

Car critics thought it would fail, but it swings big time, due in part to its entertainment system housed in a center-mounted instrument cluster with 9 speakers. Its impressive dimensions—rear legroom of 38 inches and rear headroom of 45.7 inches in a vehicle that is only 155 inches long in total—make it hip to be square.

Fold down the rear seats and create 43 cubic feet of cargo room in which to execute The Swing (pictured). The man positions himself comfortably within its generous proportions. He lies semi-upright, propped up by his arms. The woman kneels astride him, her back to his stomach, and gently lowers herself into position. She then leans forward, and... oh, what a feeling!

MAJOR HAZARD Scion means descendant, of course, so to avoid the risk of conceiving one in your xB, always practice safe sex. The fully customizable Scion might encourage you to do some carmic customization of your own. Feel free—but make sure your partner is as up for improvisation as you are.

Tips >

> Access to the cargo area is facilitated via the electric solenoid-released hatch.
> Given how spacious the Scion is, the woman will find little anchorage in the car itself. She should grip her partner's shins or ankles to help her control pace and depth.

Positions >

If you triumph with **The Swing (as shown)**, try:
♥ Sporting of the Swan
♥ The Top
♥ Carma's Wheel
♥ Snake Trap

3.14 (A) Rear swaybars and a first-aid kit are supplied, but they will (hopefully) be unnecessary. **(B)** iPod friendly, with CD and dual-DVD entertainment systems to go.

Wagon's Roll: Dodge Magnum

 Precautions: This is the Soccer Mom's favorite ride, so clear out all sports equipment, especially smelly post-game gear, and make sure no small child is still hiding in back.

The Dodge Magnum is a sports wagon, or "sports tourer" according to Dodge. Combining old-school station wagon capacity and SUV muscle without the gas-guzzling, it is the low-slung crossover star of the carpool. It is huge: 16 feet 6 inches long, with a gigantic back seat. All seats are 2 inches higher than standard, making it easier to get in and out. The cargo area is 27.3 cubic feet, opening to 72 cubic feet when the back seat is folded forward into the floor.

Depending on how hectic your day shapes up to be, you can enjoy being either a slow touring type or a suitably sporty rider. For the former, both partners stretch out across the back seat, side by side, turned toward each other with legs outstretched. The woman raises her uppermost leg and bends it over his, allowing entry. This is the Fifth Posture (pictured); it allows deep penetration and leads to long, slow, langorous lovemaking. It's really easy to lose all sense of time, so avoid this position if you are on the school run and have a tight schedule.

Alternatively, if you are fit and bounding with carmic energy, try the Pounding on the Spot, which is best performed with the back seats folded flat. The man sits with his legs outstretched, facing toward the rear to avoid head-butting the low tapering roof. The woman sits astride him, wrapping her legs and arms around him. He can use his hands to help her movements. (It is much like horseback riding, which involves the same thigh muscles.)

Things can get very physical when performing Pounding on the Spot, but fortunately the Magnum includes a small removable cooler with its own electrical supply, tucked into the left-hand side of the cargo area; keep this stocked up with chilled drinks for afterward.

MAJOR HAZARD Although the Magnum's interior space and versatility make it great for carmic activity, it may be hard to find a time when it is not full of Little Leaguers or junior soccer teams. During summer camp, perhaps?

Positions >

The Magnum's specifications make it ideal for a range of the more athletic carmic positions, so feel free to improvise:
- ♥ Pounding on the Spot
- ♥ **The Fifth Posture (as shown)**
- ♥ Raised Feet
- ♥ Rainbow Arch

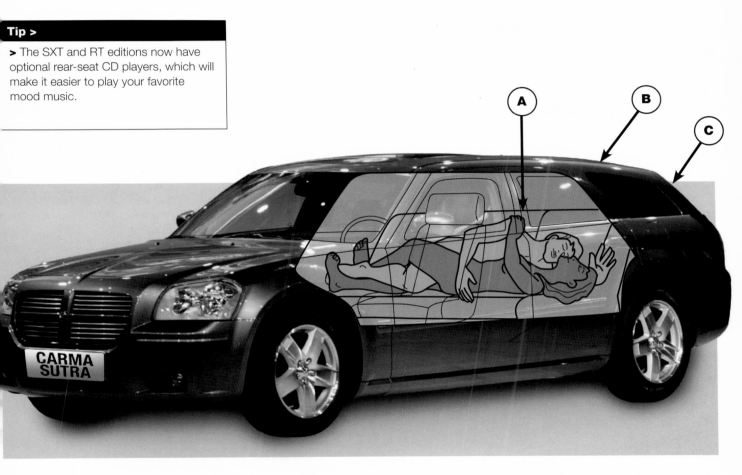

3.15 (A) Spacious back seat (74 inches wide, 40.2 inches of legroom, 4.8 inches knee clearance); **(B)** a tapering roofline restricts headroom in cargo area. **(C)** The hatchback gate is hinged about 2 feet into the roof, so it can be opened for extra room.

Sutra Utility Vehicle: Toyota Sequoia

⚠️ **Precautions:** The third-row seat in the Sequoia has legroom of 29.8 inches and hiproom of 50.3 inches per rider. It can seat three, but it is a tight squeeze. You could use the third row to get things warmed up, but it might be best to stick to the second row once things get up and running.

The Sequoia is a gas-loving, full-size SUV (maximum 18 mpg), but since it has room for eight, consider splitting fuel costs, with fellow partiers. Privacy glass all around (except the front windows) comes standard, and both basic SR5 and Limited versions offer optional load-leveling rear suspension. The fixed cup holders in front and back are designed to grip whatever is put in them, so there is no risk of spillage.

For group fun, you may prefer to stay with the basic SR5, as both rows of back seats are bench style. Use them as they are, or tumble the middle row of seats forward to create more room on the back seat. You can also push the middle seats into the recline position for a more luxurious ride, but this prevents anyone else from using the back row.

In the Limited version, the middle row comprises twin bucket seats, so riders are restricted to front seat positions (*see page 24*). On the plus side, the Limited has an electronically operated sun/moonroof over the front seats, so driver and passenger can enjoy kneeling positions such as the Raised Feet position, since headroom won't be a problem.

The Sequoia has heat-reflecting windows and automatic climate control, so head to the desert and try Cicada on a Bough (pictured on either row of the back seats (or the cargo area, or in the space created when the middle seats are folded down). The woman lies on her front and the man stretches out along her body with his knees between hers. She can raise herself on her elbows if she likes, or lay flat and breathe in the heady aroma of the Limited version's real leather upholstery.

An alternative is Carma's Wheel. The man sits upright with his legs stretched out and parted. The woman sits on him, face-to-face, stretching her legs over his and behind his body. They hold each other with outstretched arms, to make the eight-spoke wheel pattern that symbolizes kama.

Tip >

> If you plan to go for an audacious space-consuming carmic maneuver such as Carma's Wheel, remove the third row of seats before you go anywhere. They do not fold away, so they'll have to be unbolted from the floor with handtools and stored in your garage.

Positions >

Take advantage of the bench-style seats to perform:
- ♥ **Cicada on a Bough (as shown)**
- ♥ Carma's Wheel
- ♥ The Transverse Lute

MAJOR HAZARD Do not fill the car up with so many people that you have to bring the luggage in a trailer. Research suggests that the Sequoia handles best when not towing heavy loads.

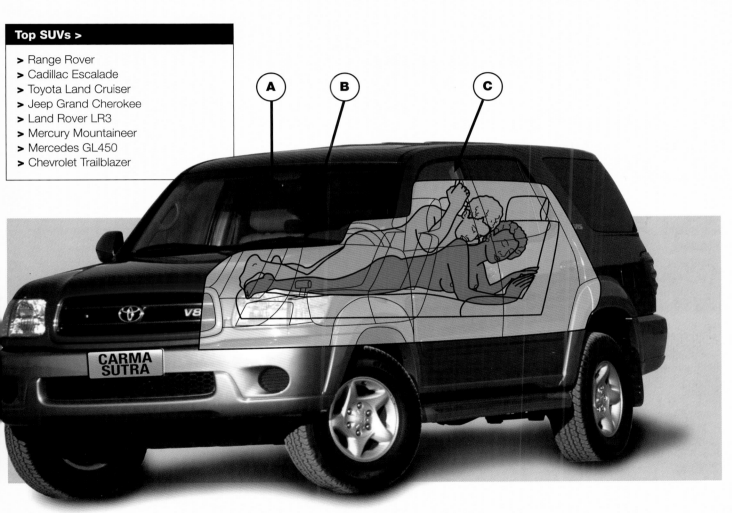

Top SUVs >

> Range Rover
> Cadillac Escalade
> Toyota Land Cruiser
> Jeep Grand Cherokee
> Land Rover LR3
> Mercury Mountaineer
> Mercedes GL450
> Chevrolet Trailblazer

3.16 (A) Heat-reflecting privacy glass; **(B)** automated climate control; **(C)** grab handles for leverage.

4. Maintenance and Troubleshooting

This final section offers tips on maintenance for you and your car, and advice on what to do when things go wrong. Sex and driving your car are both much more enjoyable when all the parts are functioning optimally.

Modern engines are designed to have fewer maintenance requirements and longer service intervals, so you don't need to worry about the serious stuff under the hood. The Essential Maintenance section covers the parts that impact on carmic maneuvers, especially the electric systems, fluids and hydraulics, brakes, chassis integrity, and suspension. The last thing you want is for the electric windows to seize and trap a vital body part, or for your shocks to buckle under heavy action.

The maintenance section also covers your own body. Really exhilarating carmic action requires supple limbs, flexible joints, upper body strength, stamina, the ability to recover quickly from cramped muscles, and mental focus. Follow our hints and tips on the kind of exercise routines that will help, and the healthy eating approach that will put you in top carmic health. A list of effective nutritional supplements is also supplied.

Of course, nobody's perfect so Essential Maintenance is followed by a Troubleshooting section. Here, we list the most common problems that drivers and lovers experience, and offer solutions to prevent embarrassment, or the end of what was once a beautiful affair. This section is designed to be used as a quick-fix repair guide only; you should always take the car or yourself in for a examination by a professional when necessary.

Essential Maintenance

⚠️ Precautions: People, just like their cars, need regular checkups and maintenance. Age, make, and model should to be taken into account on both scores, but you can extend your carmic days by keeping yourself in peak condition. Follow our advice for bumper-to-bumper fitness.

Fuel

The right fuel—appropriate and performance-enhancing—should be administered or engines could stall at crucial moments. You rely on your vehicle and your body to get you from A to B, and you should respect the needs of both. You don't knowingly fill your car with junk do you? So don't do the same to your own energy tanks. Five portions of fruit and vegetables daily and a balanced diet, low in fat, junk-food, and alcohol, are essential for the successful practice of *Carma Sutra*. It's the equivalent of filling your automobile with the right fuel for its specifications. Using cod liver oil can increase joint flexibility. Like engine oil, it can keep parts and joints running smoothly. Remember, you get out what you put in, so don't let your performance flag because of poor maintenance.

Tune-ups

Establish a preventive checklist for external and internal working parts—yours and those of your car. Get regular tune-ups to ensure that oil, water, brake fluid, windshield washer fluid, tires, lights, and airbags are in tip-top shape. Look underneath the vehicle for loose or damaged parts or corrosion. You may be giving your suspension a run for its money, so make sure that it is up to it. Ask the professionals if in doubt. You go to the doctor, so why shouldn't your car?

Pre-date Checklist

☐ Check that the alarm system is in full working order and that *Carma Sutra* activity in a parked vehicle will not trigger it.

☐ While running back and forth between front seat and back seat, be careful not to lock yourselves out of the car. Either disengage the auto-locks or keep your keys handy.

☐ Make sure the parking brake is fully engaged or you could find yourself unexpectedly advancing or reversing in a non auto-erotic way.

Fitness

Research has shown that people in good physical shape enjoy better sex. If you improve your muscle strength and control, and your general flexibility, you will benefit from enhanced performance and greater safety during *Carma Sutra*. Flexible muscles and joints, a strong back and abdomen, together with precision body control, will help you execute the more advanced, demanding positions with greater ease and more intense pleasure. It's a win–win situation.

Carmic exercise

Exercise is good for body, mind, and soul. It improves your physique and stamina, gives you a better self-image, and is a mood enhancer. All that serotonin makes you feel good about yourself, better about your body, and more inclined toward love. It can raise your libido and counteract some dysfunctions by encouraging blood flow to vital parts.

You don't have to join a gym. Regular walks, aerobic exercise, yoga and Pilates, even belly-dancing or salsa classes—all these can help. Try exercising with your lover. Get hot and sweaty before you embark on your *Carma Sutra* program and you will enjoy the ride even more.

Mind, bodywork, spirit

Pilates can really increase your carmic flexibility. Its creator, Joseph Hubertus Pilates, wanted his exercise to improve all facets of life, including sexual health, so your pelvic muscles will get a serious workout. You will gain vital core strength and stability, and master the art of engaging your pelvic floor, which will help you enjoy increased control and sensation. Yoga too is excellent for building strength and increasing flexibility. It will also clear and focus your mind, and teach you how to breathe properly.

Troubleshooting and Repairs

 Precautions: Despite your best efforts (*see page 72*), things can still go wrong. Below we list a few troubleshooting tips to help when the inevitable mechanical failure or personal dysfunction occurs.

For the car: Continuous horn

During carmic activity it's easy for one or both of you to lean on the horn. This is not a big problem unless the horn gets jammed, Here are some helpful hints:

1) Push on the horn button a few times to dislodge a stuck connection in the steering wheel.

2) Push the button while turning the wheel backward and forward.

3) Suspend carmic activity and look for the fuse box (usually below steering wheel, to the left). Find the fuse labeled "horn" and pull it. You might need needle-nosed pliers, but anyone with slender fingers should be able to pull a fuse.

4) If none of the above works, disconnect the battery's negative terminal; this means your car won't start, so make it your last resort.

False alarm

Inadvertently setting off the alarm kills the carmic mood instantly so don't try to ignore it; get out and fix it as quickly as you can:

1) Put the key in the ignition and try to start the car; on many models this shuts down the alarm.

2) Unset the alarm manually by putting the key in the lock of the passenger door, turning and holding until the alarm stops.

3) Find the fuse labeled "alarm" (see "Continuous horn"). Pull it out. If the alarm was an add-on, the fuse will be under the hood, usually on a wire connected to the positive battery terminal. It will not be labeled. Better to leave this job to a mechanic.

4) If none of the above works, disconnect the battery's negative terminal.

Tip >

> Many problems can be avoided with the correct lubrication. Always keep a can of 3-in-I oil handy in the glove compartment in case seat belt buckles seize up. Don't forget your personal lubricant of choice, plus a pack of wipes or tissues, as well.

WARNING >

> Under no circumstances should inexperienced people attempt any under-the-hood work—especially in the dark!

Parking brake seizure

The parking brake should be engaged, but if one of you pulls on it while performing front seat maneuvers, it may get stuck (because you probably won't have pressed the release button). If you cannot make it go down again, try pressing the button while pulling the lever. If this does not work and you are not far from home, drive home carefully. The parking brake works on the rear wheels, but will not hold against an accelerating vehicle. There will be a terrible smell of burning rubber, you will have to have the whole thing fixed, and maybe the tires replaced, but it may be worth it to avoid calling AAA to fix the brake cable.

For yourselves: Sluggish start

Like an engine, the libido does not always start at once, especially in cold conditions. Don't be afraid to let things idle for a time before you begin. Play your favorite music, relax, and stick to kissing, embracing, and light scratching (see page 22) until you pick up speed.

Piston misfire

Sometimes your timing just goes, and nothing follows the correct sequence. Don't panic; just take your mind off the job. Think of dull things. Memorize your license number, vehicle identification number, and the recommended tire pressures, and repeat them slowly to yourself. If that fails, get out your car manual and read it over your partner's shoulder (why else do you keep it in the glove box?) until you get things back under control.

Dead battery

This malfunction is usually reported by women. It can happen if you've been overdoing it, or even if you haven't. Inability to climax can also occur if you always park in the same place, in the same car, and always use the same position. Introduce variations into your Carma Sutra routine and try out positions that offer more stimulation of the G spot, such as Raised Feet (see page 19). Avoid stop–start relationships that can drain your sexual drive.

Famous Carma Sutra Models

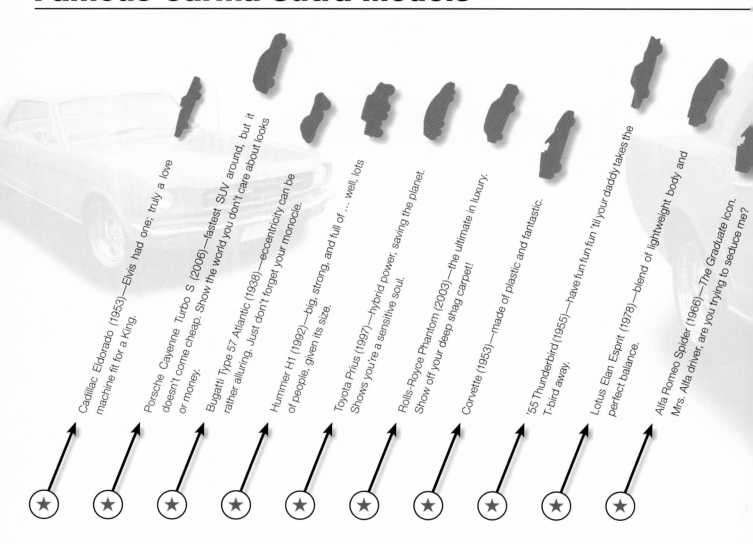

Cadillac Eldorado (1953)—Elvis had one; truly a love machine fit for a King.

Porsche Cayenne Turbo S (2006)—fastest SUV around, but it doesn't come cheap. Show the world you don't care about looks or money.

Bugatti Type 57 Atlantic (1938)—eccentricity can be rather alluring. Just don't forget your monocle.

Hummer H1 (1992)—big, strong, and full of … well, lots of people, given its size.

Toyota Prius (1997)—hybrid power, saving the planet. Shows you're a sensitive soul.

Rolls-Royce Phantom (2003)—the ultimate in luxury. Show off your deep shag carpet!

Corvette (1953)—made of plastic and fantastic.

'55 Thunderbird (1955)—have fun fun fun 'til your daddy takes the T-bird away.

Lotus Elan Esprit (1978)—blend of lightweight body and perfect balance.

Alfa Romeo Spider (1966)—The Graduate icon. Mrs. Alfa driver, are you trying to seduce me?

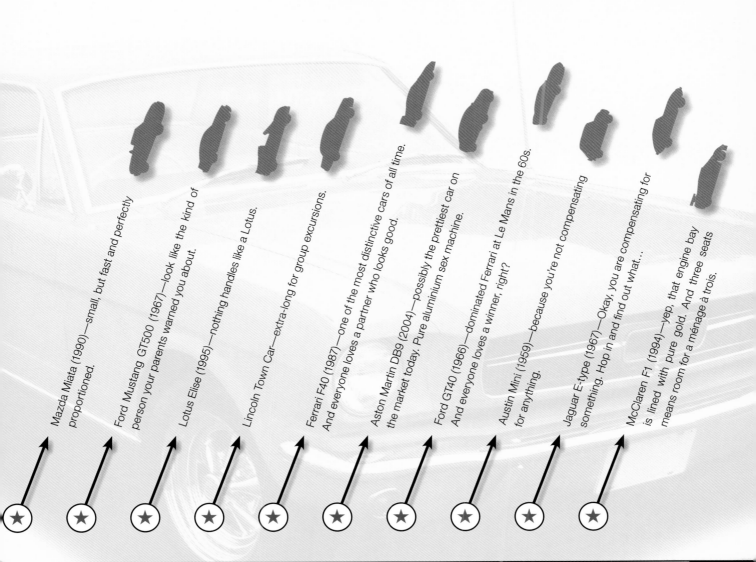

Mazda Miata (1990)—small, but fast and perfectly proportioned.

Ford Mustang GT500 (1967)—look like the kind of person your parents warned you about.

Lotus Elise (1995)—nothing handles like a Lotus.

Lincoln Town Car—extra-long for group excursions.

Ferrari F40 (1987)—one of the most distinctive cars of all time. And everyone loves a partner who looks good.

Aston Martin DB9 (2004)—possibly the prettiest car on the market today. Pure aluminium sex machine.

Ford GT40 (1966)—dominated Ferrari at Le Mans in the 60s. And everyone loves a winner, right?

Austin Mini (1959)—because you're not compensating for anything.

Jaguar E-type (1967)—Okay, you are compensating for something. Hop in and find out what...

McClaren F1 (1994)—yep, that engine bay is lined with pure gold. And three seats means room for a ménage à trois.

Index

Acknowledgments

The publisher would like to thank the following organizations and individuals for permission to reproduce the photographs in this book. Every effort has been made to acknowledge the pictures, however we apologize if there are any unintentional omissions.

Alamy/Ace Stock Limited: 31; Mark Scheuern: 35, 55, 65; Motoring Picture Library: 59; PCL: gatefold 1, 3; Phil Talbot: front cover, 63; Pixonnet.com: 61; Transtock Inc.: 1, 33, 45, 49, 51, 69

Corbis/Bettmann: 41; Cathrine Wessel: 36; Jim Zuckerman: 70; John Hillery: 47; Rick Gomez: gatefold 2, 7; Royalty-Free: 8

Getty Images: back cover, 43, 53, 67

Murray Jackson: gatefold 1, p7

Simon Punter: 39